Fifth Edition

NorthStar 3

Reading & Writing

Authors: Laurie Barton
           Carolyn Dupaquier

Series Editors: Frances Boyd
                  Carol Numrich

Dedication

To Natasha and Madeline, to whom I hope will see the world.
—Laurie Barton

I would like to dedicate this edition to my children, Alexander and Alyse Sardinas, who let me work and never complained.
—Carolyn Dupaquier

NorthStar: Reading & Writing Level 3, Fifth Edition

Copyright © 2020, 2015, 2009, 2004 by Pearson Education, Inc.
All rights reserved.

No part of this publication may be reproduced, stored in a retrieval system, or transmitted in any form or by any means, electronic, mechanical, photocopying, recording, or otherwise, without the prior permission of the publisher.

Pearson Education, 221 River St, Hoboken, NJ 07030

Staff credits: The people who made up the *NorthStar: Reading & Writing Level 3, Fifth Edition* team, representing content creation, design, manufacturing, marketing, multimedia, project management, publishing, rights management, and testing, are Pietro Alongi, Stephanie Callahan, Gina DiLillo, Tracey Cataldo, Dave Dickey, Warren Fishbach, Sarah Hand, Lucy Hart, Gosia Jaros-White, Stefan Machura, Linda Moser, Dana Pinter, Karen Quinn, Katarzyna Starzynska - Kosciuszko, Paula Van Ells, Claire Van Poperin, Joseph Vella, Peter West, Autumn Westphal, Natalia Zaremba, and Marcin Zimny.

Project consultant: Debbie Sistino
Text composition: ElectraGraphics, Inc.
Development editing: Andrea Bryant
Cover design: Studio Montage

Library of Congress Cataloging-in-Publication Data

A Catalog record for the print edition is available from the Library of Congress.

Printed in the United States of America

ISBN-13: 978-0-13-523263-7 (Student Book with Digital Resources)
ISBN-10: 0-13-523263-5 (Student Book with Digital Resources)

ISBN-13: 978-0-13-522699-5 (Student Book with MyEnglishLab Online Workbook and Resources)
ISBN-10: 0-13-522699-6 (Student Book with MyEnglishLab Online Workbook and Resources)

2 2019

CONTENTS

WELCOME TO NORTHSTAR

A Letter from the Series Editors

We welcome you to the 5th edition of *NorthStar Reading & Writing Level 3*.

Engaging content, integrated skills, and critical thinking continue to be the touchstones of the series. For more than 20 years *NorthStar* has engaged and motivated students through contemporary, authentic topics. Our online component builds on the last edition by offering new and updated activities.

Since its first edition, *NorthStar* has been rigorous in its approach to critical thinking by systematically engaging students in tasks and activities that prepare them to move into high-level academic courses. The cognitive domains of Bloom's taxonomy provide the foundation for the critical thinking activities. Students develop the skills of analysis and evaluation and the ability to synthesize and summarize information from multiple sources. The capstone of each unit, the final writing or speaking task, supports students in the application of all academic, critical thinking, and language skills that are the focus of unit.

The new edition introduces additional academic skills for 21st century success: note-taking and presentation skills. There is also a focus on learning outcomes based on the Global Scale of English (GSE), an emphasis on the application of skills, and a new visual design. These refinements are our response to research in the field of language learning in addition to feedback from educators who have taught from our previous editions.

NorthStar has pioneered and perfected the blending of academic content and academic skills in an English Language series. Read on for a comprehensive overview of this new edition. As you and your students explore *NorthStar*, we wish you a great journey.

Carol Numrich and Frances Boyd, the editors

New for the FIFTH EDITION

New and Updated Themes

The new edition features one new theme per level (i.e., one new unit per book), with updated content and skills throughout the series. Current and thought-provoking topics presented in a variety of genres promote intellectual stimulation. The real-world-inspired content engages students, links them to language use outside the classroom, and encourages personal expression and critical thinking.

Learning Outcomes and Assessments

All unit skills, vocabulary, and grammar points are connected to GSE objectives to ensure effective progression of learning throughout the series. Learning outcomes are present at the opening and closing of each unit to clearly mark what is covered in the unit and encourage both pre- and post-unit self-reflection. A variety of assessment tools, including online diagnostic, formative, and summative assessments and a flexible gradebook aligned with clearly identified unit learning outcomes, allow teachers to individualize instruction and track student progress.

Note-Taking as a Skill in Every Unit

Grounded in the foundations of the Cornell Method of note-taking, the new note-taking practice is structured to allow students to reflect on and organize their notes, focusing on the most important points. Students are instructed, throughout the unit, on the most effective way to apply their notes to a classroom task, as well as encouraged to analyze and reflect on their growing note-taking skills.

Explicit Skill Instruction and Fully-Integrated Practice

Concise presentations and targeted practice in print and online prepare students for academic success. Language skills are highlighted in each unit, providing students with multiple, systematic exposures to language forms and structures in a variety of contexts. Academic and language skills in each unit are applied clearly and deliberately in the culminating writing or presentation task.

Scaffolded Critical Thinking

Activities within the unit are structured to follow the stages of Bloom's taxonomy from *remember* to *create*. The use of APPLY throughout the unit highlights culminating activities that allow students to use the skills being practiced in a free and authentic manner. Sections that are focused on developing critical thinking are marked with 🔍 to highlight their critical focus.

Explicit Focus on the Academic Word List

AWL words are highlighted at the end of the unit and in a master list at the end of the book.

The Pearson Practice English App

The **Pearson Practice English App** allows students on the go to complete vocabulary and grammar activities, listen to audio, and watch video.

ExamView

ExamView Test Generator allows teachers to customize assessments by reordering or editing existing questions, selecting test items from a bank, or writing new questions.

MyEnglishLab

New and revised online supplementary practice maps to the updates in the student book for this edition.

THE NORTHSTAR UNIT

1 FOCUS ON THE TOPIC

Each unit begins with an eye-catching unit opener spread that draws students into the topic. The learning outcomes are written in simple, student-friendly language to allow for self-assessment. Focus on the Topic questions connect to the unit theme and get students to think critically by making inferences and predicting the content of the unit.

UNIT 1

Sports and Obsession

1 FOCUS ON THE TOPIC

1. What sport is this person doing?
2. What kind of person participates in this type of sport?
3. How are extreme sports different from other sports?

LEARNING OUTCOMES

> Infer certainty
> Take notes on key words and phrases
> Recognize quotations and reported speech

> Use modals of ability
> Add information for clarity
> Write a factual report

Go to **MyEnglishLab** to check what you know.

2 UNIT 1

Sports and Obsession 3

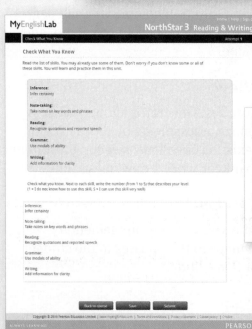

MyEnglishLab

The "Check What You Know" pre-unit diagnostic checklist provides a short self-assessment based on each unit's GSE-aligned learning outcomes to support the students in building an awareness of their own skill levels and to enable teachers to target instruction to their students' specific needs.

2 FOCUS ON READING

A vocabulary exercise introduces words that appear in the readings, encourages students to guess the meanings of the words from context, and connects to the theme presented in the final writing task.

Go to MyEnglishLab lines indicate when additional practice is available online.

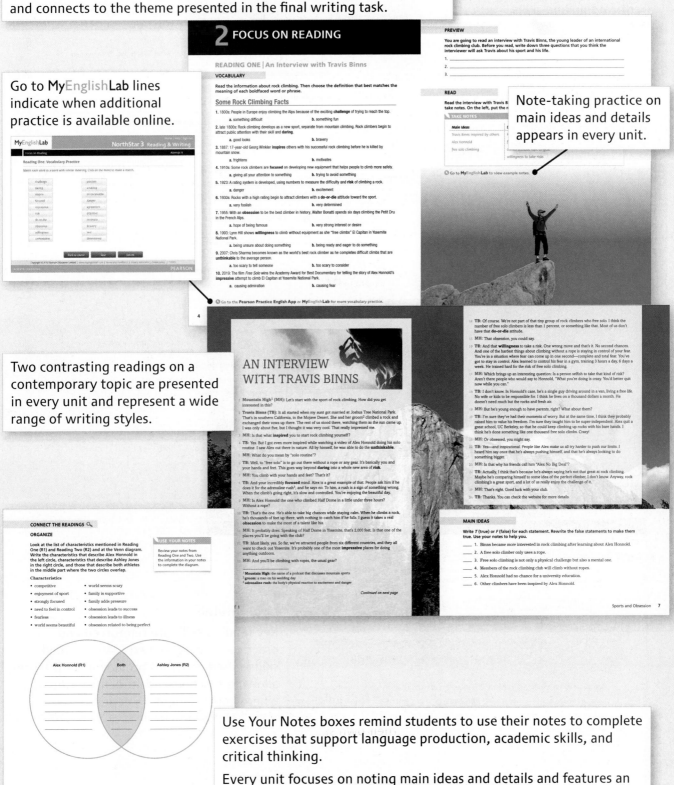

Two contrasting readings on a contemporary topic are presented in every unit and represent a wide range of writing styles.

Note-taking practice on main ideas and details appears in every unit.

Use Your Notes boxes remind students to use their notes to complete exercises that support language production, academic skills, and critical thinking.

Every unit focuses on noting main ideas and details and features an additional note-taking skill applicable to the readings.

EXPLICIT SKILL INSTRUCTION AND PRACTICE

Step-by-step instructions and practice guide students to move beyond the literal meaning of the text. 🔍 highlights activities that help build critical thinking skills.

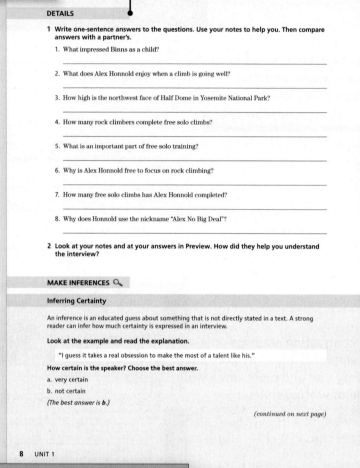

DETAILS

1 Write one-sentence answers to the questions. Use your notes to help you. Then compare answers with a partner's.

1. What impressed Binns as a child?
   _____

2. What does Alex Honnold enjoy when a climb is going well?
   _____

3. How high is the northwest face of Half Dome in Yosemite National Park?
   _____

4. How many rock climbers complete free solo climbs?
   _____

5. What is an important part of free solo training?
   _____

6. Why is Alex Honnold free to focus on rock climbing?
   _____

7. How many free solo climbs has Alex Honnold completed?
   _____

8. Why does Honnold use the nickname "Alex No Big Deal"?
   _____

2 Look at your notes and at your answers in Preview. How did they help you understand the interview?

MAKE INFERENCES 🔍

Inferring Certainty

An inference is an educated guess about something that is not directly stated in a text. A strong reader can infer how much certainty is expressed in an interview.

Look at the example and read the explanation.

"I guess it takes a real obsession to make the most of a talent like his."

How certain is the speaker? Choose the best answer.

a. very certain

b. not certain

*(The best answer is **b**.)*

(continued on next page)

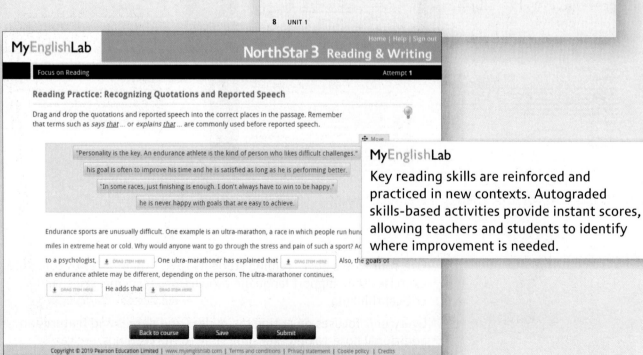

MyEnglishLab
Key reading skills are reinforced and practiced in new contexts. Autograded skills-based activities provide instant scores, allowing teachers and students to identify where improvement is needed.

3 FOCUS ON WRITING

Productive vocabulary targeted in the unit is reviewed, expanded upon, and used creatively.

Grammar presentations focus on skills that are used in the readings and applied in the final writing task. A concise grammar skills box serves as a reference point for students throughout the unit and beyond.

MyEnglishLab

Auto-graded vocabulary and grammar practice activities reinforce meaning, form, and function. Meaningful and instant feedback guides students to self-correct and provides students and teachers with essential information to monitor progress.

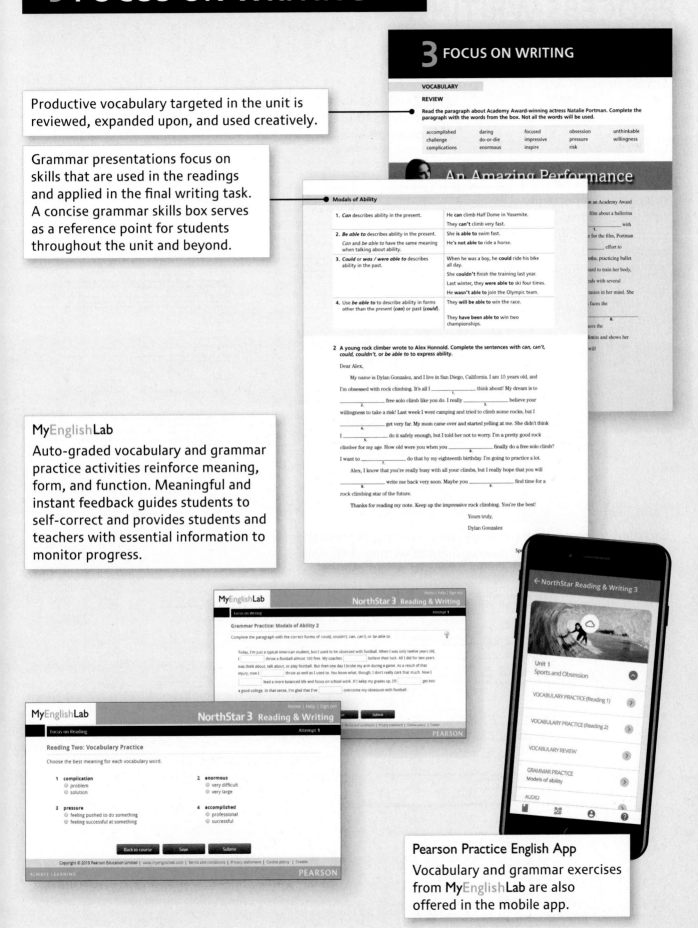

Pearson Practice English App

Vocabulary and grammar exercises from MyEnglishLab are also offered in the mobile app.

A TASK-BASED APPROACH TO PROCESS WRITING

APPLY calls out activities that get students to use new skills in a productive task.

A final writing task gives students an opportunity to integrate ideas, vocabulary, and grammar presented in the unit.

---

3 **APPLY** Write five statements about yourself, each using a different verb expressing ability from the box. Write some statements that are true and some statements that are false. Exchange papers with a classmate. Guess which statements are true and which are false.

| be able to | not be able to | can | can't | could | couldn't |

Go to the **Pearson Practice English App** or **My**English**Lab** for more grammar practice. Check what you learned in **My**English**Lab**.

FINAL WRITING TASK: A Factual Report 🔍 **APPLY**

In this unit, you read about Alex Honnold, a rock climber who is famous for his free solo climbs.

Now imagine that you are a newspaper reporter. You are going to *write a factual report of one paragraph about another amazing rock climbing achievement of Alex Honnold's: the completion of the Triple.* You may want to consider these questions as you write your report.

What was he able to do?

How quickly could he do it?

How can he take such risks?

For an alternative writing topic, see page 25.

PREPARE TO WRITE: Group Brainstorming

1 Work in a small group. Write brainstorming questions you would want to ask Alex Honnold about his completion of the Triple. Think of as many questions as you can and write them down. Do not worry about spelling and grammar.

Brainstorming Questions

2 Share your questions with the class. Your teacher will write the questions on the board.

20   UNIT 1

WRITE

Using the 5 Ws to Write a Factual Report

A news article is an example of a factual report. Good newspaper articles answer five basic questions—called the 5Ws. The answers to these questions will give you key information for your factual report.

- **Who** is the story about?
- **What** is the story about?
- **When** did the story take place?
- **Where** did the story take place?
- **Why** or **How** did the story happen?

In a factual report, quotations (people's exact words) may also be used to give more facts.

1 Look back at the newspaper article in Reading Two. How is it different from the style of Reading One? What do you think is the purpose of the newspaper article?

2 Go back to the interview in Reading One. Notice how the reporter asks questions to learn information about Alex Honnold, including his climb of Half Dome. Write five questions you would like to ask Honnold about completing the Triple, using the 5Ws.

1. Who _____
2. What _____
3. When _____
4. Where _____
5. Why / How _____

3 Look at the facts about Alex Honnold's climb. Match them with the correct questions. You may use a question more than once.

Questions

a. What was Honnold able to do all by himself?
b. What is the Triple?
c. When was Honnold able to complete the Triple?
d. Where did he do it?
e. How quickly could he do it?
f. Why is this climb so impressive?

Facts

___ 1. Alex Honnold made history when he completed the Triple.

___ 2. Climbing the Triple includes climbing three very large rock surfaces in Yosemite Park: Mount Watkins, El Capitan, and Half Dome.

___ 3. Very few climbers in the world can complete this 7,000-foot climb in 24 hours.

___ 4. The Triple is located in one of Honnold's favorite climbing spots, Yosemite National Park in California.

___ 5. On Mount Watkins, Honnold was able to keep his balance even while climbing with insects that covered his ears, neck, and mouth.

Sports and Obsession   21

Each unit presents different stages of the writing process and encourages the structured development of writing skills both practical and academic.

___ 6. As he completed the Triple in June 2012, crowds of people waited to congratulate him.

___ 7. During most of the climb, Honnold used no rope at all.

___ 8. Honnold was able to complete the Triple in record time: 18 hours and 50 minutes.

___ 9. It would only take one mistake for Honnold to fall and die.

___ 10. Honnold was the first climber who was able to complete the Triple alone.

4 Plan the first draft of your paragraph by completing the outline. Use the 5Ws information to explain how Alex Honnold was able to complete the Triple.

1. Begin with a sentence that states the **main idea** of your paragraph.

2. Give at least five supporting details (based on the 5Ws).

3. End with a sentence that restates the **main idea** of the paragraph in a new way.

5 Look at your outline and your notes from Prepare to Write, page 20, and Organize, page 14. Write the first draft of your paragraph.

- Make sure you have a strong main idea.
- Include five or more supporting details based on the 5Ws.
- End with a sentence that restates the main idea.
- Use modals to show ability.

22   UNIT 1

REVISE: Adding Information for Clarity

1 Read the sentence and problem below. Then read the revised sentence and underline the information that has been added.

- **Sentence:** Vista High School gymnast Ashley Jones was hospitalized Tuesday for complications related to anorexia nervosa.
- **Problem:** Some people may not know what anorexia nervosa is.
- **Revised sentence:** Vista High School gymnast Ashley Jones was hospitalized Tuesday for complications related to anorexia nervosa, a disorder in which the person is obsessed with dieting.

Adding Information for Clarity

When you write, think about your **audience**, the people who will read what you write. Remember that they may know less about the topic than you do. Make sure you clearly explain new words or expressions. There are several ways to **add more information** to a sentence:

1. Add more information, between commas, **in the middle** of the sentence.

Dr. Paula Kim, *director of the Eating Disorders Clinic at Baldwin Hospital*, explains that it is not unusual for athletes to become obsessed with their weight.

2. Add more information after a comma **at the end** of the sentence.

She explains that an obsession with weight can lead to extreme dieting, *which affects not only the body but also the mind.*

2 Read the paragraph. The underlined words need more explanation. Use the explanations that follow to rewrite the sentences. Compare your answers with a partner's.

According to ANRED, eating disorders continue to be on the rise among athletes, especially in sports that emphasize being thin. Sports such as gymnastics, figure skating, dancing, and synchronized swimming have a higher percentage of athletes with eating disorders. According to an American College of Sports Medicine study, eating disorders affected 62 percent of the females in these sports. Christy Henrich died of anorexia in 1994. Anorexia nervosa affects about 1 percent of female adolescents in the United States. Bulimia nervosa affects about 4 percent of college-aged women. If you want more information, contact the NEDIC.

a. ANRED = Anorexia Nervosa and Related Eating Disorders, an organization that provides information about eating disorders

b. Christy Henrich = a top United States gymnast in the late 1980s

c. anorexia nervosa = an eating disorder that makes people stop eating because they believe they are fat and want to be thin

d. bulimia nervosa = an eating disorder in which people cannot stop themselves from eating too much and then vomit in order to control their weight

e. NEDIC = National Eating Disorder Information Center

Sports and Obsession   23

X   The NorthStar Unit

Students continue through the writing process to learn revision techniques that help them move toward coherence and unity in their writing. Finally, students edit their work with the aid of a checklist that focuses on essential outcomes.

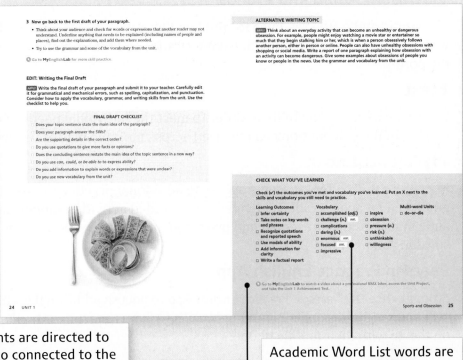

At the end of the unit, students are directed to MyEnglishLab to watch a video connected to the theme, access the Unit Project, and take the Unit Achievement Test.

Academic Word List words are highlighted with **AWL** at the end of the unit.

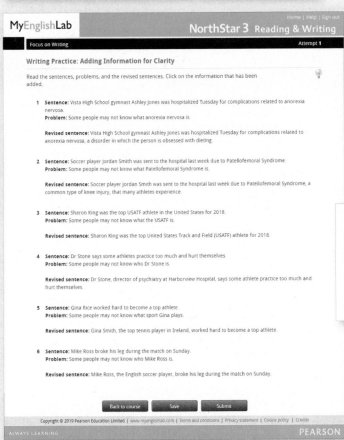

MyEnglishLab
Key writing skills and strategies are reinforced and practiced in new contexts. Autograded skills-based activities provide instant scores, allowing teachers and students to identify where improvement is needed.

COMPONENTS

Students can access the following resources on the Pearson English Portal.

- **Classroom Audio and Videos**

  Classroom audio (the readings for the Reading & Writing strand and the listenings and exercises with audio for the Listening & Speaking strand) and the end-of-unit videos are available on the portal.

- **Etext**

  Offering maximum flexibility in order to meet the individual needs of each student, the digital version of the student book can be used across multiple platforms and devices.

- **MyEnglishLab**

  MyEnglishLab offers students access to additional practice online in the form of both auto-graded and teacher-graded activities. Auto-graded activities support and build on the academic and language skills presented and practiced in the student book. Teacher-graded activities include speaking and writing.

- **Pearson Practice English App**

  Students use the Pearson Practice English App to access additional grammar and vocabulary practice, audio for the listenings and readings from the student books, and the end-of-unit videos on the go with their mobile phone.

INNOVATIVE TEACHING TOOLS

With instant access to a wide range of online content and diagnostic tools, teachers can customize learning environments to meet the needs of every student. Digital resources, all available on the Pearson English Portal, include **MyEnglishLab** and ExamView.

Using MyEnglishLab, *NorthStar* teachers can

Deliver rich online content to engage and motivate students, including

- student audio to support listening and speaking skills, in addition to audio versions of all readings.
- engaging, authentic video clips tied to the unit themes.
- opportunities for written and recorded reactions to be submitted by students.

Use diagnostic reports to

- view student scores by unit, skill, and activity.
- monitor student progress on any activity or test as often as needed.
- analyze class data to determine steps for remediation and support.

Access Teacher Resources, including

- unit teaching notes and answer keys.
- downloadable diagnostic, achievement and placement tests, as well as unit checkpoints.
- printable resources including lesson planners, videoscripts, and video activities.
- classroom audio.

Using ExamView, teachers can customize Achievement Tests by

- reordering test questions.
- editing questions.
- selecting questions from a bank.
- writing their own questions.

SCOPE AND SEQUENCE

	1 Sports and Obsession Pages: 2–25 Reading 1: An Interview with Travis Binns Reading 2: High School Star Hospitalized for Eating Disorder	**2 The Consequences of Fraud** Pages: 26–49 Reading 1: Catch Me If You Can: The Frank Abagnale Story Reading 2: The Michelle Brown Story: Identity Theft
Inference	Inferring certainty	Inferring comparisons
Note-Taking	Taking notes on key words and phrases	Taking notes with questions
Reading	Recognizing quotations and reported speech	Identifying detailed examples
Grammar	Modals of ability	Simple past and past progressive
Revise	Adding information for clarity	Using topic sentences
Final Writing Task	A factual report	A descriptive paragraph
Video	A professional BMX Biker	Identity theft

Assessments	Pre-Unit Diagnostic:
	   Check What You Know
	Checkpoint 1
	Checkpoint 2
	Unit Achievement Test
		Pre-Unit Diagnostic:
		   Check What You Know
		Checkpoint 1
		Checkpoint 2
		Unit Achievement Test

Unit Project	Write a factual report about the life and accomplishments of an athlete	Conduct research and write a report on fraud

3 Exploring the Red Planet	4 Language and Power
Pages: 50–73 Reading 1: Mars: Our New Home? Reading 2: Timeline for a Mission to Mars	Pages: 74–97 Reading 1: Men, Women, and Language Reading 2: The Question of Global English
Inferring degrees of difficulty	Inferring meaning of proverbs
Marking a text	Taking notes with a T-chart
Scanning for details	Recognizing how examples support opinions
Infinitives of purpose	Comparative adverbs
Using parallel structure	Using transitions of contrast
A pro and con paragraph	A contrast paragraph
Space	Language

Pre-Unit Diagnostic:
   Check What You Know
Checkpoint 1
Checkpoint 2
Unit Achievement Test
	Pre-Unit Diagnostic:
	   Check What You Know
	Checkpoint 1
	Checkpoint 2
	Unit Achievement Test

Write a report about a mission to Mars	Conduct research and write a report about a language

SCOPE AND SEQUENCE

	5 Careers of the Future Pages: 98–123 Reading 1: Meet Your New Boss: You Reading 2: Great Jobs for the Twenty-first Century	**6 What is Ecotourism?** Pages: 124–145 Reading 1: Tourist in a Fragile Land Reading 2: A Travel Journal
Inference	Inferring when humor is used	Inferring probability
Note-Taking	Taking notes with bullets	Taking notes on supporting details
Reading	Predicting content from titles and subheadings	Using context clues to understand vocabulary
Grammar	Future time clauses	*Because* and *even though*
Revise	Following cover letter format	Choosing effective supporting details
Final Writing Task	A cover letter	An opinion essay
Video	Careers	Ecotourism

Assessments	Pre-Unit Diagnostic:
	   Check What You Know
	Checkpoint 1
	Checkpoint 2
	Unit Achievement Test
		Pre-Unit Diagnostic:
		   Check What You Know
		Checkpoint 1
		Checkpoint 2
		Unit Achievement Test

Unit Project	Create a job posting for a fictional job using a guide to include necessary information	Write a report on an organization working to save the environment

7 Capital Punishment	8 Is Our Climate Changing?
Pages: 146–175 Reading 1: Life in Prison is Still Life: Why Should a Killer Live? / Why Do We Kill People to Show That Killing People is Wrong? Reading 2: Charts: Global Facts About Capital Punishment	Pages: 176–203 Reading 1: Global Climate Change Reading 2: Solving The Problems of Climate Change
Inferring both sides of a debate	Inferring purpose
Taking notes with an outline	Taking notes with symbols
Identifying key information in charts	Identifying cohesive devices of contrast
Adverb clauses of concession	Future modals
Using sentence variety	Using conjunctions and transitions to show cause and effect
An opinion essay	A cause-and-effect essay
The death penalty	Family living
Pre-Unit Diagnostic: 　Check What You Know Checkpoint 1 Checkpoint 2 Unit Achievement Test	Pre-Unit Diagnostic: 　Check What You Know Checkpoint 1 Checkpoint 2 Unit Achievement Test
Use questions to guide research on a specific country's use of capital punishment, write a summary and share findings with class	Research and create a presentation about climate change

ACKNOWLEDGMENTS

Many people helped in the creative process that resulted in this book. We are grateful to Allen Ascher, who first gave us this opportunity, and to everyone at Pearson who has contributed to the *NorthStar* series. To Debbie Sistino, who so graciously and efficiently organized the 1st–4th editions, providing clear direction and guidance, many thanks. To Peter West and all who worked so hard on the 5th edition, more thanks. Most of all, we want to express our deep appreciation to our series editors, Frances Boyd and Carol Numrich. Their insight into what students need to progress, and the grace they've extended to us from the beginning, will never be forgotten.

—Laurie Barton and Carolyn Dupaquier

REVIEWERS

Chris Antonellis, Boston University – CELOP; Gail August, Hostos; Aegina Barnes, York College; Kim Bayer, Hunter College; Mine Bellikli, Atilim University; Allison Blechman, Embassy CES; Paul Blomquist, Kaplan; Helena Botros, FLS; James Branchick, FLS; Chris Bruffee, Embassy CES; Joyce Cain University of California at Fullerton; Nese Cakli, Duzce University; Molly Cheny, University of Washington; María Cordani Tourinho Dantas, Colégio Rainha De Paz; Jason Davis, ASC English; Lindsay Donigan, Fullerton College; Mila Dragushanskaya, ASA College; Bina Dugan, BCCC; Sibel Ece Izmir, Atilim University; Érica Ferrer, Universidad del Norte; María Irma Gallegos Peláez, Universidad del Valle de México; Vera Figueira, UC Irvine; Rachel Fernandez, UC Irvine; Jeff Gano, ASA College; Emily Ellis, UC Irvine; María Genovev a Chávez Bazán, Universidad del Valle de México; Juan Garcia, FLS; Heidi Gramlich, The New England School of English; Phillip Grayson, Kaplan; Rebecca Gross, The New England School of English; Rick Guadiana, FLS; Sebnem Guzel, Tobb University; Esra Hatipoglu, Ufuk University; Brian Henry, FLS; Josephine Horna, BCCC; Judy Hu, UC Irvine; Arthur Hui, Fullerton College; Zoe Isaacson, Hunter College; Kathy Johnson, Fullerton College; Marcelo Juica, Urban College of Boston; Tom Justice, North Shore Community College; Lisa Karakas, Berkeley College; Eva Kopernacki, Embassy CES; Drew Larimore, Kaplan; Heidi Lieb, BCCC; Patricia Martins, Ibeu; Cecilia Mora Espejo, Universidad del Valle de México; Oscar Navarro University of California at Fullerton; Eva Nemtson, ASA College; Kate Nyhan, The New England School of English; Julie Oni, FLS; Willard Osman, The New England School of English; Olga Pagieva, ASA College; Manish Patel, FLS; Paige Poole, Universidad del Norte; Claudia Rebello, Ibeu; Amy Renehan, University of Washington; Lourdes Rey, Universidad del Norte; Michelle Reynolds, FLS International Boston Commons; Mary Ritter, NYU; Ellen Rosen University of California at Fullerton; Dana Saito-Stehiberger, UC Irvine; Dariusz Saczuk, ASA College; Miryam Salimov, ASA College; Minerva Santos, Hostos; Sezer Sarioz, Saint Benoit PLS; Gail Schwartz, UC Irvine; Ebru Sinar, Tobb University; Beth Soll, NYU (Columbia); Christopher Stobart, Universidad del Norte; Guliz Uludag, Ufuk University; Debra Un, NYU; Hilal Unlusu, Saint Benoit PLS; María del Carmen Viruega Trejo, Universidad del Valle de México; Reda Vural, Atilim University; Douglas Waters, Universidad del Norte; Emily Wong, UC Irvine; Leyla Yucklik, Duzce University; Jorge Zepeda Porras, Universidad del Valle de México

LEARNING OUTCOMES

> Infer certainty
> Take notes on key words and phrases
> Recognize quotations and reported speech

> Use modals of ability
> Add information for clarity
> Write a factual report

Go to **MyEnglishLab** to check what you know.

Sports and Obsession

1 FOCUS ON THE TOPIC

1. What sport is this person doing?
2. What kind of person participates in this type of sport?
3. How are extreme sports different from other sports?

VOCABULARY

Read the information about rock climbing. Then choose the definition that best matches the meaning of each boldfaced word or phrase.

Some Rock Climbing Facts

1. 1800s: People in Europe enjoy climbing the Alps because of the exciting **challenge** of trying to reach the top.

    a. something difficult   **b.** something fun

2. late 1800s: Rock climbing develops as a new sport, separate from mountain climbing. Rock climbers begin to attract public attention with their skill and **daring**.

    a. good looks   **b.** bravery

3. 1887: 17-year-old Georg Winkler **inspires** others with his successful rock climbing before he is killed by mountain snow.

    a. frightens   **b.** motivates

4. 1910s: Some rock climbers are **focused** on developing new equipment that helps people to climb more safely.

    a. giving all your attention to something   **b.** trying to avoid something

5. 1923: A rating system is developed, using numbers to measure the difficulty and **risk** of climbing a rock.

    a. danger   **b.** excitement

6. 1930s: Rocks with a high rating begin to attract climbers with a **do-or-die** attitude toward the sport.

    a. very foolish   **b.** very determined

7. 1955: With an **obsession** to be the best climber in history, Walter Bonatti spends six days climbing the Petit Dru in the French Alps.

    a. hope of being famous   **b.** very strong interest or desire

8. 1993: Lynn Hill shows **willingness** to climb without equipment as she "free climbs" El Capitan in Yosemite National Park.

    a. being unsure about doing something   **b.** being ready and eager to do something

9. 2007: Chris Sharma becomes known as the world's best rock climber as he completes difficult climbs that are **unthinkable** to the average person.

    a. too scary to tell someone   **b.** too scary to consider

10. 2019: The film *Free Solo* wins the Academy Award for Best Documentary for telling the story of Alex Honnold's **impressive** attempt to climb El Capitan at Yosemite National Park.

    a. causing admiration   **b.** causing fear

Go to the **Pearson Practice English App** or **MyEnglishLab** for more vocabulary practice.

PREVIEW

You are going to read an interview with Travis Binns, the young leader of an international rock climbing club. Before you read, write down three questions that you think the interviewer will ask Travis about his sport and his life.

1. _____

2. _____

3. _____

READ

Read the interview with Travis Binns on the next page. Create a chart like the one below to take notes. On the left, put the main ideas. On the right, put the details.

TAKE NOTES

Main Ideas	Details
Travis Binns inspired by others	his aunt
Alex Honnold	free solo climber
free solo climbing	climbs without rope or gear
	willingness to take risks

Go to **MyEnglishLab** to view example notes.

AN INTERVIEW WITH TRAVIS BINNS

1 **Mountain High[1] (MH):** Let's start with the sport of rock climbing. How did you get interested in this?

2 **Travis Binns (TB):** It all started when my aunt got married at Joshua Tree National Park. That's in southern California, in the Mojave Desert. She and her groom[2] climbed a rock and exchanged their vows up there. The rest of us stood there, watching them as the sun came up. I was only about five, but I thought it was very cool. That really impressed me.

3 **MH:** Is that what **inspired** you to start rock climbing yourself?

4 **TB:** Yes. But I got even more inspired while watching a video of Alex Honnold doing his solo routine. I saw Alex out there in nature. All by himself, he was able to do the **unthinkable**.

5 **MH:** What do you mean by "solo routine"?

6 **TB:** Well, to "free solo" is to go out there without a rope or any gear. It's basically you and your hands and feet. This goes way beyond **daring** into a whole new area of **risk**.

7 **MH:** You climb with your hands and feet? That's it?

8 **TB:** And your incredibly **focused** mind. Alex is a great example of that. People ask him if he does it for the adrenaline rush[3], and he says no. To him, a rush is a sign of something wrong. When the climb's going right, it's slow and controlled. You're enjoying the beautiful day.

9 **MH:** Is Alex Honnold the one who climbed Half Dome in a little under three hours? Without a rope?

10 **TB:** That's the one. He's able to take big chances while staying calm. When he climbs a rock, he's thousands of feet up there, with nothing to catch him if he falls. I guess it takes a real **obsession** to make the most of a talent like his.

11 **MH:** It probably does. Speaking of Half Dome in Yosemite, that's 2,000 feet. Is that one of the places you'll be going with the club?

12 **TB:** Most likely, yes. So far, we've attracted people from six different countries, and they all want to check out Yosemite. It's probably one of the most **impressive** places for doing anything outdoors.

13 **MH:** And you'll be climbing with ropes, the usual gear?

---

[1] **Mountain High:** the name of a podcast that discusses mountain sports
[2] **groom:** a man on his wedding day
[3] **adrenaline rush:** the body's physical reaction to excitement and danger

Continued on next page

14 **TB:** Of course. We're not part of that tiny group of rock climbers who free solo. I think the number of free solo climbers is less than 1 percent, or something like that. Most of us don't have that **do-or-die** attitude.

15 **MH:** That obsession, you could say.

16 **TB:** And that **willingness** to take a risk. One wrong move and that's it. No second chances. And one of the hardest things about climbing without a rope is staying in control of your fear. You're in a situation where fear can come up in one second—complete and total fear. You've got to stay in control. Alex learned to control his fear in a gym, training 3 hours a day, 6 days a week. He trained hard for the risk of free solo climbing.

17 **MH:** Which brings up an interesting question: Is a person selfish to take that kind of risk? Aren't there people who would say to Honnold, "What you're doing is crazy. You'd better quit now while you can."

18 **TB:** I don't know. In Honnold's case, he's a single guy driving around in a van, living a free life. No wife or kids to be responsible for. I think he lives on a thousand dollars a month. He doesn't need much but the rocks and fresh air.

19 **MH:** But he's young enough to have parents, right? What about them?

20 **TB:** I'm sure they've had their moments of worry. But at the same time, I think they probably raised him to value his freedom. I'm sure they taught him to be super-independent. Alex quit a great school, UC Berkeley, so that he could keep climbing up rocks with his bare hands. I think he's done something like one thousand free solo climbs. Crazy!

21 **MH:** Or obsessed, you might say.

22 **TB:** Yes—and inspirational. People like Alex make us all try harder to push our limits. I heard him say once that he's always pushing himself, and that he's always looking to do something bigger.

23 **MH:** Is that why his friends call him "Alex No Big Deal"?

24 **TB:** Actually, I think that's because he's always saying he's not that great at rock climbing. Maybe he's comparing himself to some idea of the perfect climber, I don't know. Anyway, rock climbing's a great sport, and a lot of us really enjoy the challenge of it.

25 **MH:** That's right. Good luck with your club.

26 **TB:** Thanks. You can check the website for more details.

MAIN IDEAS

Write _T_ (true) or _F_ (false) for each statement. Rewrite the false statements to make them true. Use your notes to help you.

_____ 1. Binns became more interested in rock climbing after learning about Alex Honnold.

_____ 2. A free solo climber only uses a rope.

_____ 3. Free solo climbing is not only a physical challenge but also a mental one.

_____ 4. Members of the rock climbing club will climb without ropes.

_____ 5. Alex Honnold had no chance for a university education.

_____ 6. Other climbers have been inspired by Alex Honnold.

1 Write one-sentence answers to the questions. Use your notes to help you. Then compare answers with a partner's.

1. What impressed Binns as a child?

   _____

2. What does Alex Honnold enjoy when a climb is going well?

   _____

3. How high is the northwest face of Half Dome in Yosemite National Park?

   _____

4. How many rock climbers complete free solo climbs?

   _____

5. What is an important part of free solo training?

   _____

6. Why is Alex Honnold free to focus on rock climbing?

   _____

7. How many free solo climbs has Alex Honnold completed?

   _____

8. Why does Honnold use the nickname "Alex No Big Deal"?

   _____

2 Look at your notes and at your answers in Preview. How did they help you understand the interview?

MAKE INFERENCES 🔍

Inferring Certainty

An inference is an educated guess about something that is not directly stated in a text. A strong reader can infer how much certainty is expressed in an interview.

Look at the example and read the explanation.

"I guess it takes a real obsession to make the most of a talent like his."

How certain is the speaker? Choose the best answer.

a. very certain

b. not certain

*(The best answer is **b**.)*

(continued on next page)

When reading an interview, we can infer certainty by looking for words and phrases such as *I think, I guess, probably, most likely, maybe,* or *something like that*. All of these indicate that a speaker is **only somewhat certain** of what he or she says.

When speakers make a statement **without these kinds of words and phrases,** we infer that they are **more certain**.

Sometimes speakers use **short statements** to emphasize that they are **very certain**.

> "Most of us don't have . . . that willingness to take a risk. <u>One wrong move and that's it. No second chances.</u>"

The underlined statements are short and direct; from these short statements we can infer that the speaker is very certain of what is being said.

1 Read each statement. Choose the best answer to indicate how certain the speaker is.

1. I think the number of free solo climbers is less than 1 percent, or something like that.

   a. very certain   b. not certain

2. You're in a situation where fear can come up in one second—complete and total fear. You've got to stay in control.

   a. very certain   b. not certain

3. People like Alex make us all try harder to push our limits.

   a. very certain   b. not certain

4. Maybe he's comparing himself to some idea of the perfect climber, I don't know.

   a. very certain   b. not certain

5. I'm sure Alex's parents have had their moments of worry.

   a. very certain   b. not certain

6. But at the same time, I think they probably raised him to value his freedom.

   a. very certain   b. not certain

2 Now discuss your answers with a partner. Point out words, phrases, or statements that helped you find the answers.

DISCUSS 🔍

Work in small groups. Choose one of the questions. Discuss your ideas. Then choose one person in your group to report the ideas to the class.

> **USE YOUR NOTES**
>
> Use your notes to support your answers with information from the reading.

1. How are Travis Binns and Alex Honnold similar? How are they different?

2. Who has been affected by Alex Honnold's climbing besides Travis Binns?

3. How have Honnold's parents reacted to his rock climbing? What do you think of their reaction?

🔘 Go to **MyEnglishLab** to give your opinion about another question.

READING TWO | High School Star Hospitalized for Eating Disorder

PREVIEW

1 Look at the title and photo below. Read the first paragraph. Write two questions that you think will be answered in this reading.

_____

_____

2 Look at the boldfaced words in the reading. Which words do you know the meaning of?

READ

1 Read the article in a local newspaper about a high school gymnast. As you read, guess the meanings of the words that are new to you. Remember to take notes on main ideas and details.

High School Star Hospitalized for Eating Disorder

1 Vista High School gymnast Ashley Jones was hospitalized Tuesday for **complications** related to anorexia nervosa. Her coach, Dianne Coyle, says that she will not be returning to the gymnastics team this season.

2 "It's really a loss—not only to the team but also to Ashley personally," says Coyle. "She had hopes of qualifying for the Olympics. But her health comes first, of course. Once she is better, I'm sure she can get back into the sport and go for the gold."

3 Dr. Paula Kim, director of the Eating Disorders Clinic at Santa Anita Hospital, explains that it is not unusual for athletes, especially gymnasts, to become obsessed with their weight. One reason for this is that in gymnastics, the lighter the body, the more skillfully it can perform. She explains that an obsession with weight can lead to extreme dieting, which affects not only the body but also the mind.

4 "For the anorexic, the mental focus becomes very small: food and weight. In a way, it's easy to see how this helps the anorexic manage the fear of living in the big, uncontrollable world out there. You may not be able to control how other people feel about you, but you can control what you put in your mouth. You can also control

how many hours you spend at the gym. Soon you get hooked on controlling your weight."

5 High school counselor Lisa Rodriguez has expressed concern that Jones's illness is related to pressure.

6 "There's an **enormous** amount of **pressure** that goes along with training for the Olympics," she says. "I know that she comes from a very **accomplished** family— I think that's why she felt she had to achieve so much in sports. Also, when you talk about the Olympics, you're talking about being the best of the best. I think that added to Ashley's feeling of pressure."

7 Since joining the Vista High gymnastics team as a sophomore two years ago, Ashley has broken all school records and led the team to three regional championships.

Continued on next page

Continued on next page

8   Coach Coyle says, "As soon as I met Ashley, I could tell right away that she was obsessed with the sport. And that's not the kind of athlete that you have to push. My goal with Ashley was to try and help her have more of a balanced life. I talked to her about how she was doing in her classes, what she might want to study in college. I also told her and all the members on the team to take at least one or two days a week just to let their bodies rest. I know it's a very difficult situation, but all I can say is I'm so sorry Ashley got sick."

9   Coyle's concern for Jones's health is shared by her teammates and friends. Some of them recall how the tiny gymnastics star worked out at the health club in addition to hours of regular practice with the team. They describe how the walls of her bedroom are covered with photos of Olympic winners —Mo Huilan and Gabby Douglas to name a few.

10   Jones, who currently weighs only 72 pounds (32.6 kilograms), is expected to remain in the hospital for at least a few months.

2 Compare your notes on main ideas and details with a partner's. How can you improve your notes next time?

⟩ Go to the **Pearson Practice English App** or **MyEnglishLab** for more vocabulary practice.

NOTE-TAKING SKILL

Taking Notes on Key Words and Phrases

There are many kinds of key words and phrases. When a text has names, they are a good place to start in note taking. After you write down names, write down phrases (two to five words) that tell you more about them—places, events, and other names. Focusing on names and phrases can help you remember main points for tests and other assignments. Be sure to include the person's first and last name, along with any title that appears with the name (doctor, coach, etc.). This will help you remember who the people are and how they may be related to each other. Use dashes and parentheses to organize your notes.

Vista High School gymnast Ashley Jones was hospitalized Tuesday for complications related to anorexia nervosa. Her coach, Dianne Coyle, says that she will not be returning to the gymnastics team this season. "It's really a loss—not only to the team but also to Ashley personally," says Coyle.

Notes:

Ashley Jones—Vista HS gymnast
            —in hospital (anorexia nervosa)

Dianne Coyle—AJ's coach
            —AJ not returning to team

High school counselor Lisa Rodriguez has expressed concern that Jones's illness is related to pressure. "There's an enormous amount of pressure that goes along with training for the Olympics," she says.

Notes:

Lisa Rodriguez—AJ's counselor
            —AJ's illness related to pressure

1 **Look at the names of other people from the reading. Add phrases (two to five words) to identify main points. Share your answers with a partner.**

a. Ashley Jones—*Vista High School gymnast*_____

b. Dianne Coyle—_____

c. Dr. Paula Kim—_____

d. Lisa Rodriguez—_____

e. Mo Huilan—_____

f. Gabby Douglas—_____

2 **Look at Reading Two again and take more notes about Ashley Jones. Add more phrases about her eating disorder.**

🔊 Go to **MyEnglishLab** for more note-taking practice.

COMPREHENSION

1 **Choose the best answer to complete the statements. Use your notes from Reading Two to help you. Discuss your answers with a partner.**

1. Ashley's coach hopes that she will leave the hospital and _____ .

   a. focus on her health   b. join the Olympic team

2. According to Dr. Paula Kim, anorexia nervosa is an obsession with _____ .

   a. exercise   b. weight

3. The doctor says that one reason for becoming anorexic is that it gives a person a feeling of _____ .

   a. more control   b. mental focus

4. Some of the pressure in Ashley's life was because she wanted to be the best gymnast in _____ .

   a. her country   b. the world

5. Before she went to the hospital, Ashley's coach had been pushing her to focus on gymnastics _____ .

   a. less   b. more

2 **Review the boldfaced words from the reading with a partner. Use a dictionary or ask your teacher for any meanings you still do not know.**

READING SKILL

1 Read the statement from Reading Two. Then answer the questions.

"[Ashley] had hopes of qualifying for the Olympics. But her health comes first, of course. Once she is better, I'm sure she can get back into the sport and go for the gold."

Who is speaking here? Is it Ashley or someone else? How do we know?

Recognizing Quotations and Reported Speech

In many types of writing, both quoted speech and reported speech are used:

Quoted speech includes quotation marks to indicate that a person's exact words are being reported.

"It's really a loss—not only to the team but also to Ashley personally," says Coyle.

Reported speech does not include quotation marks and is an explanation of what someone has said. In reported speech, different words may be used to express the original meaning.

Her coach, Dianne Coyle, says that she will not be returning to the gymnastics team this season.

Most news articles include the names of several people. As you read news articles, it is important to pay attention to names of people and also to pronouns that refer to these people. This will help you to keep track of what people in the article have done and said. As a result, you will understand the article more clearly.

2 Work with a partner to answer the questions about Reading Two.

1. Read paragraph 2. Is this quoted or reported speech?
2. Whose speech is being reported in paragraph 3?
3. Read paragraph 5. Is this quoted or reported speech?
4. Who is speaking in paragraph 6?
5. Read paragraph 8. Is this quoted or reported speech?
6. In the same paragraph, who is being referred to by the pronouns *her* and *their*?

Go to **MyEnglishLab** for more skill practice.

ORGANIZE

Look at the list of characteristics mentioned in Reading One (R1) and Reading Two (R2) and at the Venn diagram. Write the characteristics that describe Alex Honnold in the left circle, characteristics that describe Ashley Jones in the right circle, and those that describe both athletes in the middle part where the two circles overlap.

USE YOUR NOTES

Review your notes from Reading One and Two. Use the information in your notes to complete the diagram.

Characteristics

- competitive
- enjoyment of sport
- strongly focused
- need to feel in control
- fearless
- world seems beautiful
- world seems scary
- family is supportive
- family adds pressure
- obsession leads to success
- obsession leads to illness
- obsession related to being perfect

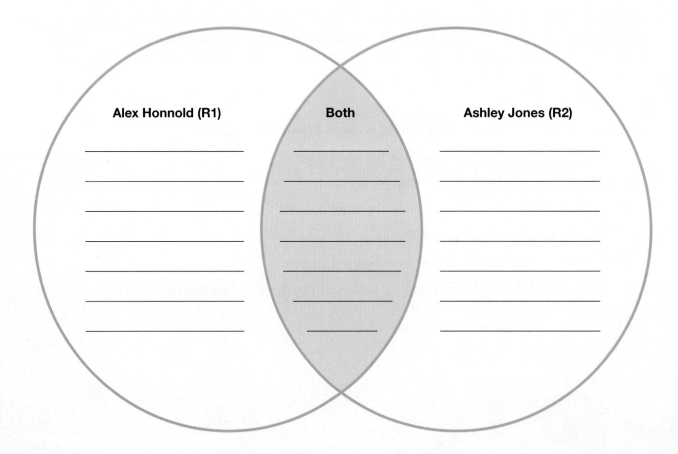

Alex Honnold (R1)　　　Both　　　Ashley Jones (R2)

SYNTHESIZE

Work with a partner. Complete the paragraph about obsession with what you know about Alex Honnold and Ashley Jones. Use your Venn diagram from Organize.

Obsession can be helpful or destructive, depending on the person. This can be clearly seen in two

examples from the sports world. Alex Honnold and Ashley Jones are both _____

_____

_____ .

In addition, _____ .

However, there are important differences between them. Alex Honnold _____

_____ .

Ashley Jones _____ .

Also, _____ .

As we look at these examples, it is interesting to see how obsession can either help or harm

a person.

🔾 Go to **MyEnglishLab** to check what you learned.

VOCABULARY

REVIEW

Read the paragraph about Academy Award-winning actress Natalie Portman. Complete the paragraph with the words from the box. Not all the words will be used.

accomplished	daring	focused	obsession	unthinkable
challenge	do-or-die	impressive	pressure	willingness
complications	enormous	inspire	risk	

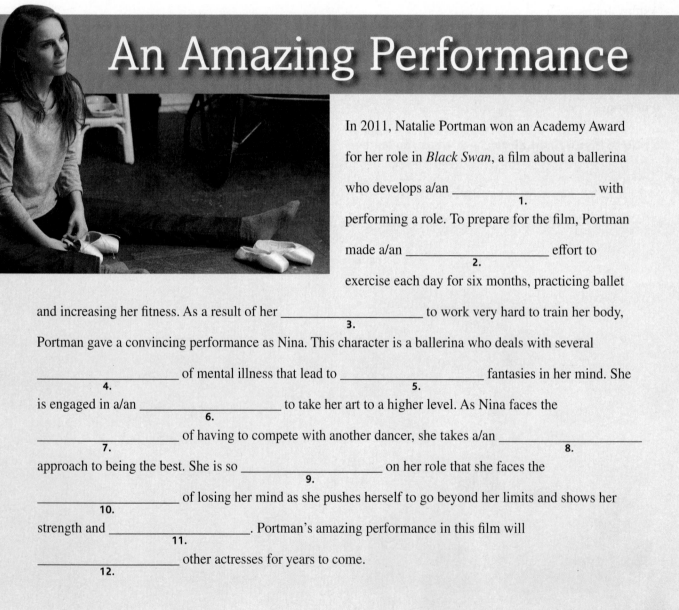

An Amazing Performance

In 2011, Natalie Portman won an Academy Award for her role in *Black Swan*, a film about a ballerina who develops a/an _____ with
1.
performing a role. To prepare for the film, Portman made a/an _____ effort to
2.
exercise each day for six months, practicing ballet and increasing her fitness. As a result of her _____ to work very hard to train her body,
3.
Portman gave a convincing performance as Nina. This character is a ballerina who deals with several _____ of mental illness that lead to _____ fantasies in her mind. She
4.   5.
is engaged in a/an _____ to take her art to a higher level. As Nina faces the
6.
_____ of having to compete with another dancer, she takes a/an _____
7.   8.
approach to being the best. She is so _____ on her role that she faces the
9.
_____ of losing her mind as she pushes herself to go beyond her limits and shows her
10.
strength and _____. Portman's amazing performance in this film will
11.
_____ other actresses for years to come.
12.

EXPAND

Complete the chart with the correct word forms. Some categories can have more than one form. Use a dictionary if necessary. An X indicates that you do not need to put a form in that category.

	NOUN	VERB	ADJECTIVE	ADVERB
1.	accomplishment		accomplished	X
2.	challenge			X
3.	complication			X
4.	a. daring b.			
5.		X	enormous	
6.			focused	X
7.			impressive	
8.		inspire		
9.	obsession		a. b. obsessive	
10.	pressure			X
11.	risk			X
12.	willingness	X		

CREATE

APPLY Write a paragraph describing one of your achievements, hobbies, or goals. Use at least five of the words from the box. You may change the form of the words.

accomplished	daring	focused	obsession	unthinkable
challenge	do-or-die	impressive	pressure	willingness
complications	enormous	inspire	risk	

Go to the **Pearson Practice English App** or **MyEnglishLab** for more vocabulary practice.

GRAMMAR FOR WRITING

1 **Look at the examples from Reading Two. Circle the boldfaced words, which are modals. Underline the verbs that follow. How do the modals change the meanings of the verbs?**

- As soon as I met Ashley, I **could** tell right away that she was obsessed with the sport.

- You may not **be able to** control how other people feel about you, but you can control what you put in your mouth.

- You **can** also control how many hours you spend at the gym.

Modals of Ability

1. *Can* describes ability in the present.	He **can** climb Half Dome in Yosemite.
	They **can't** climb very fast.
2. *Be able to* describes ability in the present.	She **is able to** swim fast.
Can and *be able to* have the same meaning when talking about ability.	He**'s not able to** ride a horse.
3. *Could* or *was / were able to* describes ability in the past.	When he was a boy, he **could** ride his bike all day.
	She **couldn't** finish the training last year.
	Last winter, they **were able to** ski four times.
	He **wasn't able to** join the Olympic team.
4. Use *be able to* to describe ability in forms other than the present (*can*) or past (*could*).	They **will be able to** win the race.
	They **have been able to** win two championships.

2 **A young rock climber wrote to Alex Honnold. Complete the sentences with *can*, *can't*, *could*, *couldn't*, or *be able to* to express ability.**

Dear Alex,

My name is Dylan Gonzalez, and I live in San Diego, California. I am 15 years old, and

I'm obsessed with rock climbing. It's all I _____ think about! My dream is to
1.

_____ free solo climb like you do. I really _____ believe your
2. 3.

willingness to take a risk! Last week I went camping and tried to climb some rocks, but I

_____ get very far. My mom came over and started yelling at me. She didn't think
4.

I _____ do it safely enough, but I told her not to worry. I'm a pretty good rock
5.

climber for my age. How old were you when you _____ finally do a free solo climb?
6.

I want to _____ do that by my eighteenth birthday. I'm going to practice a lot.
7.

Alex, I know that you're really busy with all your climbs, but I really hope that you will

_____ write me back very soon. Maybe you _____ find time for a
8. 9.

rock climbing star of the future.

Thanks for reading my note. Keep up the impressive rock climbing. You're the best!

Yours truly,

Dylan Gonzalez

3 APPLY **Write five statements about yourself, each using a different verb expressing ability from the box. Write some statements that are true and some statements that are false. Exchange papers with a classmate. Guess which statements are true and which are false.**

be able to	not be able to	can	can't	could	couldn't

> Go to the **Pearson Practice English App** or **MyEnglishLab** for more grammar practice. Check what you learned in **MyEnglishLab**.

FINAL WRITING TASK: A Factual Report 🔍 APPLY

In this unit, you read about Alex Honnold, a rock climber who is famous for his free solo climbs.

Now imagine that you are a newspaper reporter. You are going to *write a factual report of one paragraph about another amazing rock climbing achievement of Alex Honnold's: the completion of the Triple.* You may want to consider these questions as you write your report.

What was he able to do?

How quickly could he do it?

How can he take such risks?

For an alternative writing topic, see page 25.

PREPARE TO WRITE: Group Brainstorming

1 Work in a small group. Write brainstorming questions you would want to ask Alex Honnold about his completion of the Triple. Think of as many questions as you can and write them down. Do not worry about spelling and grammar.

Brainstorming Questions

_____

_____

_____

_____

_____

_____

_____

2 Share your questions with the class. Your teacher will write the questions on the board.

WRITE

Using the 5 Ws to Write a Factual Report

A news article is an example of a factual report. Good newspaper articles answer five basic questions—called the 5Ws. The answers to these questions will give you key information for your factual report.

- **Who** is the story about?
- **What** is the story about?
- **When** did the story take place?
- **Where** did the story take place?
- **Why** or **How** did the story happen?

In a factual report, quotations (people's exact words) may also be used to give more facts.

1 Look back at the newspaper article in Reading Two. How is it different from the style of Reading One? What do you think is the purpose of the newspaper article?

2 Go back to the interview in Reading One. Notice how the reporter asks questions to learn information about Alex Honnold, including his climb of Half Dome. Write five questions you would like to ask Honnold about completing the Triple, using the 5Ws.

1. **Who** _____

2. **What** _____

3. **When** _____

4. **Where** _____

5. **Why / How** _____

3 Look at the facts about Alex Honnold's climb. Match them with the correct questions. You may use a question more than once.

Questions	
a. What was Honnold able to do all by himself?	d. Where did he do it?
b. What is the Triple?	e. How quickly could he do it?
c. When was Honnold able to complete the Triple?	f. Why is this climb so impressive?

Facts

_____ 1. Alex Honnold made history when he completed the Triple.

_____ 2. Climbing the Triple includes climbing three very large rock surfaces in Yosemite Park: Mount Watkins, El Capitan, and Half Dome.

_____ 3. Very few climbers in the world can complete this 7,000-foot climb in 24 hours.

_____ 4. The Triple is located in one of Honnold's favorite climbing spots, Yosemite National Park in California.

_____ 5. On Mount Watkins, Honnold was able to keep his balance even while climbing with insects that covered his ears, neck, and mouth.

_____ 6. As he completed the Triple in June 2012, crowds of people waited to congratulate him.

_____ 7. During most of the climb, Honnold used no rope at all.

_____ 8. Honnold was able to complete the Triple in record time: 18 hours and 50 minutes.

_____ 9. It would only take one mistake for Honnold to fall and die.

_____ 10. Honnold was the first climber who was able to complete the Triple alone.

4 **Plan the first draft of your paragraph by completing the outline. Use the 5Ws information to explain how Alex Honnold was able to complete the Triple.**

1. Begin with a sentence that states the **main idea** of your paragraph.

_____

_____

2. Give at least five supporting details (based on the 5Ws).

_____

_____

_____

_____

_____

_____

3. End with a sentence that restates the **main idea** of the paragraph in a new way.

_____

_____

5 **Look at your outline and your notes from Prepare to Write, page 20, and Organize, page 14. Write the first draft of your paragraph.**

- Make sure you have a strong main idea.

- Include five or more supporting details based on the 5Ws.

- End with a sentence that restates the main idea.

- Use modals to show ability.

REVISE: Adding Information for Clarity

1 **Read the sentence and problem below. Then read the revised sentence and underline the information that has been added.**

- **Sentence:** Vista High School gymnast Ashley Jones was hospitalized Tuesday for complications related to anorexia nervosa.

- **Problem:** Some people may not know what anorexia nervosa is.

- **Revised sentence:** Vista High School gymnast Ashley Jones was hospitalized Tuesday for complications related to anorexia nervosa, a disorder in which the person is obsessed with dieting.

Adding Information for Clarity

When you write, think about your **audience,** the people who will read what you write. Remember that they may know less about the topic than you do. Make sure you **clearly explain new words or expressions.** There are several ways to **add more information to a sentence:**

1. Add more information, between commas, **in the middle** of the sentence.

> Dr. Paula Kim, *director of the Eating Disorders Clinic at Baldwin Hospital*, explains that it is not unusual for athletes to become obsessed with their weight.

2. Add more information after a comma **at the end** of the sentence.

> She explains that an obsession with weight can lead to extreme dieting, *which affects not only the body but also the mind.*

2 **Read the paragraph. The underlined words need more explanation. Use the explanations that follow to rewrite the sentences. Compare your answers with a partner's.**

> According to ANRED, eating disorders continue to be on the rise among athletes, especially in sports that emphasize being thin. Sports such as gymnastics, figure skating, dancing, and synchronized swimming have a higher percentage of athletes with eating disorders. According to an American College of Sports Medicine study, eating disorders affected 62 percent of the females in these sports. Christy Henrich died of anorexia in 1994. Anorexia nervosa affects about 1 percent of female adolescents in the United States. Bulimia nervosa affects about 4 percent of college-aged women. If you want more information, contact the NEDIC.

a. ANRED = Anorexia Nervosa and Related Eating Disorders, an organization that provides information about eating disorders

b. Christy Henrich = a top United States gymnast in the late 1980s

c. anorexia nervosa = an eating disorder that makes people stop eating because they believe they are fat and want to be thin

d. bulimia nervosa = an eating disorder in which people cannot stop themselves from eating too much and then vomit in order to control their weight

e. NEDIC = National Eating Disorder Information Center

3 Now go back to the first draft of your paragraph.

- Think about your audience and check for words or expressions that another reader may not understand. Underline anything that needs to be explained (including names of people and places), find out the explanations, and add them where needed.

- Try to use the grammar and some of the vocabulary from the unit.

🔾 Go to **MyEnglishLab** for more skill practice.

EDIT: Writing the Final Draft

APPLY Write the final draft of your paragraph and submit it to your teacher. Carefully edit it for grammatical and mechanical errors, such as spelling, capitalization, and punctuation. Consider how to apply the vocabulary, grammar, and writing skills from the unit. Use the checklist to help you.

FINAL DRAFT CHECKLIST

☐ Does your topic sentence state the main idea of the paragraph?

☐ Does your paragraph answer the 5Ws?

☐ Are the supporting details in the correct order?

☐ Do you use quotations to give more facts or opinions?

☐ Does the concluding sentence restate the main idea of the topic sentence in a new way?

☐ Do you use *can, could,* or *be able to* to express ability?

☐ Do you add information to explain words or expressions that were unclear?

☐ Do you use new vocabulary from the unit?

ALTERNATIVE WRITING TOPIC

APPLY Think about an everyday activity that can become an unhealthy or dangerous obsession. For example, people might enjoy watching a movie star or entertainer so much that they begin stalking him or her, which is when a person obsessively follows another person, either in person or online. People can also have unhealthy obsessions with shopping or social media. Write a report of one paragraph explaining how obsession with an activity can become dangerous. Give some examples about obsessions of people you know or people in the news. Use the grammar and vocabulary from the unit.

CHECK WHAT YOU'VE LEARNED

Check (✔) the outcomes you've met and vocabulary you've learned. Put an X next to the skills and vocabulary you still need to practice.

Learning Outcomes
- ☐ Infer certainty
- ☐ Take notes on key words and phrases
- ☐ Recognize quotations and reported speech
- ☐ Use modals of ability
- ☐ Add information for clarity
- ☐ Write a factual report

Vocabulary
- ☐ accomplished (*adj.*)
- ☐ challenge (*n.*) AWL
- ☐ complications
- ☐ daring (*n.*)
- ☐ enormous AWL
- ☐ focused AWL
- ☐ impressive
- ☐ inspire
- ☐ obsession
- ☐ pressure (*n.*)
- ☐ risk (*n.*)
- ☐ unthinkable
- ☐ willingness

Multi-word Units
- ☐ do-or-die

▶ Go to **MyEnglishLab** to watch a video about a professional BMX biker, access the Unit Project, and take the Unit 1 Achievement Test.

LEARNING OUTCOMES

> Infer comparisons
> Take notes with questions
> Identify detailed examples

> Use simple past and past progressive
> Use topic sentences
> Write a descriptive paragraph

 Go to **MyEnglishLab** to check what you know.

The Consequences of Fraud

1 FOCUS ON THE TOPIC

1. Look at the picture and the title of the unit. What does fraud mean? What do you think this unit will discuss?

2. There are many types of fraud. Some examples are identity theft[1], internet fraud, and medical fraud. What are some other kinds of fraud? What kinds of fraud do you think are the most common?

3. Besides financial gain, what are some other reasons people might commit fraud?

---

[1] **identity theft:** a type of fraud in which a person's identification and other information are used by a criminal, usually to open new bank accounts or credit cards and buy things with the victim's money

VOCABULARY

1 Read the article about fraud. Pay attention to the boldfaced words.

TYPES OF FRAUD

Fraud continues to increase quickly due to constantly changing technology. One example is the Grandparent Scam. An elderly person is contacted over the phone by a person who says he or she is friends with or knows the elderly person's grandchild. The caller uses social media to find out some details that make the story **convincing**. The caller says the grandchild is very sick, or in the hospital, or traveling far away and needs money immediately. The real **motive** might be to get money or to obtain personal banking information.

INTERNET FRAUD

Another type of computer fraud is known as "phishing," or trying to obtain financial information by **impersonating** a bank employee. One common way we see this type of fraud is in email messages from someone pretending to represent your bank. You are then asked to provide your account number or other identifying information. This kind of **deception** seems so real that people often respond to it and give away their financial and personal information.

We also see men and women who **con** people by calling them on the phone to offer amazing prizes. After they **impress** people, they ask for their banking information saying that they can put prize money directly into their accounts. If you do not trust a person contacting you by phone, ask for his or her name, business phone number, and company email address. You can then contact the company yourself to learn whether or not you have reason to be **suspicious**.

Technology has made it easier for people to trick you with **fake** deals and requests for information. In addition, when you go online for important matters, such as legal and medical advice, you have to be especially careful about the sites you visit and the information they provide. How can you know if you are getting real and accurate information? Fortunately, there are organizations that can help you identify and report fraud and make sure you are being treated with **honesty**. If you believe you are involved in a case of fraud, be sure to report it and ask for help.

2 Choose the correct answer to complete the definition of each boldfaced word.

1. **Fraud** is a trick to get _____ .

   a. money or power   b. computers

2. If a person is **convincing**, he or she is _____ .

   a. strong   b. believable

3. A person's **motive** for doing something is his or her _____ .

   a. reason   b. reward

4. If you **impersonate** a bank employee, you _____ .

   a. really are one   b. are pretending to be one

5. When **deception** takes place, people _____ .

   a. tell the truth   b. lie

6. A person who **cons** you is trying to _____ .

   a. trick you   b. help you

7. When someone **impresses** you, you feel _____ .

   a. amazed   b. pressured

8. When you are **suspicious** of people, you _____ .

   a. believe them   b. don't believe them

9. A **fake** deal is one that is _____ .

   a. real   b. not real

10. When people treat you with **honesty**, they are telling you _____ .

   a. the truth   b. lies

Go to the **Pearson Practice English App** or **MyEnglishLab** for more vocabulary practice.

PREVIEW

You are going to read the true story of Frank Abagnale, a man who once conned many people. Before you read, look at the list. Check (✓) three types of fraud that you think you might read about in the story.

☐ 1. impersonation   ☐ 4. internet fraud

☐ 2. telephone fraud   ☐ 5. document fraud

☐ 3. selling fake products   ☐ 6. bank fraud

READ

Read the article about Frank Abagnale. Create a chart like the one below to take notes. On the left, put the main ideas. On the right, put the details.

TAKE NOTES

Main Ideas	Details
Frank Abagnale—conned a lot of people	cashing false checks (millions of $$$)
	impersonated pilot, doctor, lawyer, professor

Go to **MyEnglishLab** to view example notes.

Catch Me If You Can: The Frank Abagnale Story

1   A doctor . . . a lawyer . . . an airline pilot . . . a college professor . . . Frank Abagnale played all these roles as a young man, **conning** people and stealing millions of dollars from banks around the world. His money-making secret? Cashing false checks. His **motive** for playing different roles? Respect and excitement. He enjoyed having other people believe that he was important.

2   He first **impersonated** an airline pilot by wearing a pilot's uniform. Then he created a phony airline ID. The result was very exciting to him. Abagnale never operated a plane, but he used his pilot uniform to fly for free and to date attractive young flight attendants. Then he discovered a luxury apartment community[1] near Atlanta, Georgia. He paid cash for six months' rent in advance and wrote "medical doctor" on his apartment application. He soon became friends with a doctor in the apartment community. After **convincing** this man that he, too, was a medical doctor, he was offered a hospital job as a temporary supervisor. Abagnale performed this role by relying on nurses and medical students to do all the work while he simply pretended to be in charge. But finally, when faced with a life-or-death situation involving a newborn baby, Abagnale decided that he could no longer continue the **deception**. He knew that if he kept impersonating a doctor, an innocent child might die. Still, before leaving his hospital job, Abagnale made sure to get his paycheck.

3   Next, he dated another flight attendant, whom he **impressed** by claiming that he had graduated from law school. She introduced him to a real lawyer, who immediately offered him a position as a state attorney. Abagnale accepted the offer, but he needed to create a **fake** transcript from Harvard Law School. He also needed to pass the state law exam. He studied for several weeks but failed the eight-hour exam on his first and second attempts. When he tried a third time, he passed and

---
[1] **luxury apartment community:** an area with very expensive and comfortable apartments

Continued on next page

became a licensed attorney despite the fact that he had never finished high school. He worked as a lawyer for nine months before he met a genuine Harvard graduate who started asking him specific questions about the school and its professors. Because Abagnale could not answer these questions, the man became **suspicious** and started questioning Abagnale's **honesty**.

4 Abagnale escaped from this uncomfortable situation by heading to the western United States. There he visited college campuses in Utah. He decided to apply for a summer teaching position, which he obtained by making a fake transcript from Columbia University and writing false letters of recommendation. Abagnale was quite happy to work as a "professor." To prepare for class, he simply used the textbook, making sure to stay one chapter ahead of the students. Abagnale also discussed his own personal experiences in class, and the students responded with much interest. But when summer school ended, he could no longer stay in Utah. He knew that the FBI was searching for him because he had been cashing phony checks all over the country. He moved to California and eventually to France, thinking he could live quietly and safely there. However, he was wrong.

5 In France, Abagnale was recognized by a flight attendant and reported to the authorities. Soon, he was in a French prison, where he almost died because of very little food and very dirty surroundings. After six months, he was sent to a prison in Sweden. He learned that police in several European countries were waiting to arrest him for check **fraud**, and he feared that prison conditions in other places might be even worse than those in France. Eventually, Sweden sent him to the United States, where he spent four years in federal prison.

6 After his release, Abagnale had a problem shared by many other criminals: limited job opportunities. He worked hard in various entry-level positions and showed the ability to become a top manager but could not get any high positions because of his prison background. He thought about returning to a life of crime but decided instead to offer his services as a "white-collar crime specialist" teaching banks and other businesses how to avoid becoming the victims of fraud. Soon he was offered a position working with the FBI Financial Crimes Unit. Today, he runs his own company. It specializes in protecting checks and other documents against fraud.

7 His first book, *Catch Me If You Can*, was made into a Steven Spielberg film in 2002. In one interview, he was asked if he had ever thought about becoming an actor, considering his skill at impersonation, which allowed him to con so many people. The answer was no. The real Frank Abagnale is satisfied with his real life as a company owner and family man.

MAIN IDEAS

Put the events of Frank Abagnale's life in the order in which they happened (1–6). Use your notes to help you.

_4_ a. He finally succeeds in passing his law exam.

_5_ b. He moves from France to Sweden.

_6_ c. He starts his own company.

_1_ d. He impersonates an airline pilot.

_2_ e. He quits his hospital job.

_3_ f. He decides to teach a college class.

1 Choose the letter of the best answer on the right to complete each sentence on the left. Use your notes to help you.

1. Abagnale used his uniform to gain _____ .
2. He got his hospital job with the help of _____ .
3. He quit impersonating a doctor after dealing with _____ .
4. He passed his law exam after _____ .
5. He was hired as a college professor because of _____ .
6. In the United States and Europe, he made money by cheating _____ .
7. He was afraid of _____ .
8. When he left prison, he was unable to get _____ .
9. Today he is employed as _____ .
10. He thought about continuing his career as _____ .
11. Despite his talents, he is not interested in _____ .

a. banks

b. high-level jobs

c. fake recommendations

d. a crime expert

e. a sick baby

f. acting

g. bad prison conditions

h. a criminal

i. several attempts

j. free travel

k. a neighbor

2 Look at your notes and at your answers in Preview. How did they help you understand the article?

MAKE INFERENCES 🔍

Inferring Comparisons

An inference is an educated guess about something that is not directly stated in a text. Writers sometimes suggest comparisons without directly stating them. A strong reader can infer these comparisons by reading the text closely.

Look at the example and read the explanation.

Frank Abagnale was more successful _____ .

Choose the best way to complete the comparison statement.

a. cashing false checks

b. deceiving people in the medical world

*(The best answer is **b**.)*

In **paragraph 2,** we learn that Abagnale worked in a hospital but made <u>his own</u> decision to leave the hospital because an innocent child might die. He worked in a hospital, but he chose to leave. *(He was successful.)*

In **paragraph 4,** we learn that the FBI was searching for him because he had been cashing phony checks. *(He was not successful.)*

In **paragraph 5,** we learn that several European countries were waiting to arrest him for check fraud. *(He was not successful.)*

After reading the text closely, we **can infer** that Abagnale was more successful deceiving people in the medical world than he was at cashing false checks.

1 Choose the best way to complete each comparison statement. Look back at the paragraphs in parentheses.

1. Frank Abagnale had an easier time impressing _____ . *(paragraphs 2 and 3)*

   a. flight attendants   b. lawyers

2. Frank Abagnale was more successful at getting a job as a _____ . *(paragraphs 3 and 4)*

   a. lawyer   b. professor

3. Prison conditions were better for Frank Abagnale in _____ . *(paragraph 5)*

   a. France   b. the United States

2 Now discuss your answers with a partner. Point out words, phrases, or statements that helped you find the answers.

DISCUSS 🔍

Work in small groups. Choose one of the questions. Discuss your ideas. Then choose one person in your group to report the ideas to the class.

> **USE YOUR NOTES**
>
> Use your notes to support your answers with information from the reading.

1. Which of Abagnale's impersonations was the most dangerous to others? Why?

2. What evidence in the text shows Abagnale's intelligence?

3. Name two people that Abagnale lied to. What advantages did he gain from these lies?

🔊 Go to **MyEnglishLab** to give your opinion about another question.

READING TWO | The Michelle Brown Story: Identity Theft

PREVIEW

1 Look at the title and photo on the next page. Read the first paragraph. Write two questions that you think will be answered in this reading.

_____

_____

2 Look at the boldfaced words in the reading. Which words do you know the meaning of?

1 Read about Michelle Brown, a real woman who experienced identity theft. As you read, guess the meanings of the words that are new to you. Remember to take notes on main ideas and details.

THE MICHELLE BROWN STORY: IDENTITY THEFT

1   What would you do if you learned that your name, address, and other personal details had been stolen, and that someone was using this information to impersonate you? Most people can think of few things more frightening than this. In January 1999, Michelle Brown made just such a discovery, and her life was never the same again.

2   Michelle was an upstanding citizen in every respect. She lived in southern California, where she had a respectable job in international banking. She was a hardworking and responsible person. She began working at the age of fifteen in order to save up for her degree, which she later completed at the University of California. From the age of seventeen, she was careful to establish good credit, and she never had any problems with her finances. Most importantly, she never committed any crime.

3   A strange phone call was the first clue that something was **fishy**. Out of the blue, a representative from her bank called to ask why a payment for a Dodge Ram pickup truck was late. Michelle was confused because she hadn't purchased a vehicle. She explained that she didn't own a truck and thought it was probably just a mistake because Michelle Brown is a very common name. She gave the bank her Social Security number to prove that the late payments must be from a different Michelle Brown. But strangely, her number matched the one on the credit application. This was **astonishing**.

4   Michelle didn't yet know how serious the situation was. However, she took a series of steps to protect herself. First, she cancelled her credit cards and filed a report with the police. Then she called the Department of Motor Vehicles. She wanted to make sure that no one had copied her driver's license. It was lucky she thought to do this, because a **duplicate** copy had indeed been issued. She found out that not only was someone borrowing money in her name, but they were trying to take on her full identity.

5   Before, Michelle was stressed. Now, she was becoming scared. To calm her nerves, she called all of the major credit reporting agencies. They placed a fraud alert on her credit and promised to put together a list of her recent purchases. That way, Michelle would at least know what items were being bought. When the report came in, Michelle saw bills for liposuction[1], apartment contracts, holiday rentals, telephone bills, and more. Including the Dodge pickup truck, there was over $50,000 worth of debt in her name.

6   Michelle did everything possible to clear her name and financial record. This process was extremely time-consuming. Meanwhile, she constantly worried that she would learn of new debt. As the weeks went on, Michelle became **weary** and paranoid. She stopped eating, developed insomnia, and closed herself off from friends and family. Her relationship with her boyfriend suffered, and the pair eventually broke up. At times, Michelle even felt unsafe in her own home, because the impostor knew her address. Even the smallest sound would cause panic. She was desperate for this nightmare to end.

7   The worst moment in the ordeal was when Michelle was stopped at Los Angeles International Airport. On her way back from a trip, immigration officials

---

[1] **liposuction:** a type of cosmetic surgery in which body fat is removed

Continued on next page

pulled her aside for questioning. The woman who stole Michelle's identity had committed several crimes, mostly related to drug trafficking. As a result, Michelle was a suspect. The situation was extremely unfair. After a lot of effort, Michelle managed to convince the authorities that she was innocent. Still, the experience left her shaken because she could have been arrested and sent to jail. She decided not to risk traveling again, even though she had done nothing wrong.

8 It took Michelle years to sort out all of these problems. During this time, all she wanted was the chance to live a normal life. And as she frequently reminded people, a normal life was something she deserved. In July 2000, Michelle testified before the U.S. Senate. In her speech, she made a number of recommendations to protect victims of identity theft. She believed that the fraud alert system should be changed, and that the government should do more to help people who suffer from these types of crimes.

2 Compare your notes on main ideas and details with a partner's. How can you improve your notes next time?

🔊 Go to the **Pearson Practice English App** or **MyEnglishLab** for more vocabulary practice.

NOTE-TAKING SKILL

Taking Notes with Questions

When you take notes, it can be helpful to write questions that will help you remember what happened in a story. This will help you answer questions on tests and other assignments.

Begin with the title. Then look at the first sentence of each paragraph and turn it in into a question. Answer the questions by taking notes. As you continue, you can ask more questions about your notes. **To understand main ideas, ask yourself: Who is doing what? Why is it important?**

Who is Michelle Brown?	(single woman, late 20s, perfect credit)
What is her story?	(identity theft)
What happened on a winter day?	(message from someone at the bank)

1 Look at the first sentences of paragraphs 3–6. Write a question for each paragraph.

a) paragraph 3: <u>Why did she say there was a mistake?   (She hadn't bought a truck.)</u>

b) paragraph 4: _____

c) paragraph 5: _____

d) paragraph 6: _____

2 Ask another question or two about the notes you took for each paragraph.

a) paragraph 3: <u>What did she tell the bank officer? (She hadn't bought a truck.)</u>

<u>What kind of truck? (a new Dodge Ram pickup)</u>

b) paragraph 4: _____

c) paragraph 5: _____

d) paragraph 6: _____

3 Look at Reading Two again. Mark the information you think is most important.

🔊 Go to **MyEnglishLab** for more note-taking practice.

COMPREHENSION

1 **Read the statements and mark them *T* (true) or *F* (false). Rewrite the false statements to make them true. Use your notes from Reading Two to help you. Discuss your answers with a partner.**

_____ 1. Michelle Brown was careless with her finances.

_____ 2. After she found out about her Social Security number, she took one step to protect herself.

_____ 3. The person who stole her identity made several purchases.

_____ 4. She began selling drugs as a way of paying her bills.

_____ 5. Identity theft affected her emotionally as well as financially.

2 **Review the boldfaced words from the reading with a partner. Use a dictionary or ask your teacher for any meanings you still do not know.**

READING SKILL

1 **Read paragraph 2 of Reading Two again. How do we know Michelle was an upstanding citizen? Underline the sentences, phrases, and words that give information about how Michelle was a good citizen.**

Identifying Detailed Examples

To understand the main ideas of a text, readers need to **identify** and understand the **detailed examples** that **support and explain** these **ideas**.

Detailed examples include information about **time, place, people,** and **events**.

Main Idea   Detailed Examples

• Michelle Brown was an upstanding citizen in every respect. She began working at the age of fifteen in order to save up for her degree, which she later completed at the University of California. From the age of seventeen, she was careful to establish good credit, and she never had any problems with her finances. Most importantly, she never committed any crime.

We sometimes see signal words such as *for example, for instance, such as, including, in addition,* and *in fact* in a text. These signal words explain the connection between the ideas and the detailed examples.

Main Idea   Detailed Examples

• Michelle Brown was an upstanding citizen in every respect. *For example*, she began working at the age of fifteen in order to save up for her degree, which she later completed at the University of California. *In addition*, from the age of seventeen, she was careful to establish good credit, and she never had any problems with her finances. *In fact*, most importantly, she never committed any crime.

The first sentence expresses the main idea. The sentences that follow give detailed examples to support and explain that idea.

2 Work with a partner. Read paragraphs 4 and 5 of Reading Two again. Answer the questions.

1. **paragraph 4:** What examples are given of the steps Michelle used to protect herself?

2. **paragraph 5:** What examples of bills that weren't Michelle's are mentioned?

🔎 Go to **MyEnglishLab** for more skill practice.

CONNECT THE READINGS 🔍

ORGANIZE

Reading One (R1) and Reading Two (R2) contain information about the financial consequences of fraud. Look at the list of consequences below. Put them in the correct category by writing the letter of each consequence in the chart.

USE YOUR NOTES

Review your notes from Reading One and Two. Use the information in your notes to complete the chart.

| FINANCIAL CONSEQUENCES OF FRAUD ||
Impersonation (R1)	Identity Theft (R2)
_____	_____
_____	_____
_____	_____

a. Banks lost money as many fake checks were cashed.

b. The victim faced late bills and new debt.

c. Someone had bought a new truck with stolen credit.

d. Legal clients paid for the services of a false lawyer.

e. A hospital lost money paying out the impostor's paychecks.

f. A fraud alert was placed on the victim's credit.

SYNTHESIZE

Use the information from the chart to complete a summary about two types of fraud: impersonation and identity theft.

Fraud can often have financial consequences on more than one individual. When Frank Abagnale

impersonated a doctor, _____

_____ .

Later, when he impersonated a licensed attorney, _____

_____ .

Another consequence is that _____

_____

as Abagnale cashed false checks. There are also financial consequences when someone's identity is

stolen. For example, Michelle Brown _____

_____ .

Also, her Social Security number _____

_____ .

Because someone _____

_____ ,

she became responsible for the payments. These financial consequences can be very serious.

⊙ Go to **MyEnglishLab** to check what you learned.

REVIEW

Read the article about a man who was practicing medicine without a license. Complete the article with the words from the box. One word is not used.

astonishing	deception	fake	fraud	impersonate	suspicious
con	duplicate	fishy	honesty	motive	weary

Phony[1] Doctor Gets 12 Years in Prison

John E. Curran will spend 12 years in prison because he pretended to be a doctor. In this case of medical

_____, he lied to sick people and said that he could cure them with his "natural"
1.

medicine. To _____ a doctor, Curran bought _____
2. **3.**

medical degrees on the internet for $2,650. It was even more _____ that he received
4.

a "medical degree" in only two months. This made him seem like a real doctor. He wore a lab coat with MD[2] after

his name and checked people's blood. He told them they had cancer or other illnesses. Then he sold them

"E-Water" and "Green Drink"—two products that would cure them, he said. He also charged people $10,000 for

the use of medical treatment machines that he kept in his office. Curran impressed people with his false medical

knowledge. They were _____ of feeling sick and believed his "natural" medicine
5.

could help them. One woman, however, became _____ of Curran after paying $1,200
6.

a month for his "Green Drink." After three months, Curran refused to check her blood, and she thought this was

_____. She went to another doctor and learned that Curran's medicine was not real:
7.

it was all a _____. In court, Curran asked the judge not to give him a strong
8.

punishment. He claimed that he was acting with complete _____ and that he really
9.

wanted to help people with his medicine. He asked the judge to be kind to him. But the judge responded that

Curran's _____ was not helping people but wanting to make money. Because the
10.

judge believed that money was the reason for Curran's actions, he gave him 12 years in prison. "You are the worst

of the worst," said the judge, believing Curran to be a dangerous liar who would _____
11.

innocent people when they were most in need of help.

---

[1] **phony:** fake or false
[2] **MD:** medical doctor

EXPAND

1 Complete the chart with the correct word forms. Some categories can have more than one form. Use a dictionary if necessary. An X indicates that you do not need to put a form in that category.

	NOUN	VERB	ADJECTIVE	ADVERB
1.	X	convice	convincing	conviacaly
2.	deception	deceive	dec	deceivet
3.	a. b.		duplicate	X
4.	a. fake b.		fake	X
5.	fraud	X		
6.	honesty	X		
7.	impersonation		X	X
8.		impress		
9.	a. motive b. motivation			X

2 Rewrite the sentences by replacing the underlined word with the form in parentheses. Make any necessary changes to grammar and syntax.

1. I believe in the <u>honesty</u> of most doctors. (honest)

   <u>*I believe that most doctors are honest.*</u>

2. I had a bad experience with a man who practiced medicine <u>fraudulently</u>. (fraudulent)

   _____

3. His <u>motive</u> was making money. (motivate)

   _____

4. Not many people understood his <u>fakery</u>. (fake *n.*)

   _____

5. I wasn't the only person involved in his <u>deception</u>. (deceive)

   _____

6. He wasn't a real doctor, but he <u>impersonated</u> one well. (impersonation)

_____

7. He had <u>duplicated</u> someone else's medical license. (duplicate *n.*)

_____

8. The man who conned us told a <u>convincing</u> story. (convincingly)

_____

9. I was <u>impressed</u> by the fake doctor at first. (impressive)

_____

CREATE

APPLY Imagine that you spent a lot of money on a fraudulent product or service. Write an online review for other customers, warning them about your bad experience. Use any form of at least five new words from this unit.

Go to the **Pearson Practice English App** or **MyEnglishLab** for more vocabulary practice.

GRAMMAR FOR WRITING

1 **Read these sentences based on Frank Abagnale's story. Look at the boldfaced verbs. What is the difference between the verb forms? Notice the words in italics. How are the meanings of *when* and *while* different?**

- Frank Abagnale **was hiding** in France *when* a flight attendant **reported** him to the authorities.

- *When* he **met** the doctor who helped him, they **were** both **renting** apartments in the same community.

- *While* the FBI **was searching** for him, he **was enjoying** himself in California.

1. Use the **simple past** to talk about an event that took place at a specific point in time in the past. This event started and finished in the past; the focus of the sentence is stating the fact that it happened.	He finally **passed** the law exam.
2. Use **past progressive** (also called **past continuous**) to describe a continuous nonstop action that was in progress at a specific time in the past.* These sentences have a focus on something taking a long time. They can be used with specific time phrases: *yesterday, last night, at that time.*	**At that time**, he **was working** at a law firm.
3. Sentences with **time clauses** talk about two events that happened in the past. Time clauses start with time words including *when* and *while*. Use *when* for interrupting events. One event is interrupted / stopped because of another event. The first event is in the **past progressive**. The event that interrupts or stops it is in the **simple past**. *When* can go with either event.	I was sleeping **when** the phone rang. **When** I was sleeping, the phone rang. I was talking on the phone **when** the police arrived. **When** I was talking on the phone, the police arrived.
4. Use *when* for two events that happened at **the same time**, but one event is much shorter than the other and the longer event doesn't stop because of the shorter event. The longer event is in the **past progressive**. The shorter event is in the **simple past**. *When* can go with either event.	I was listening to music **when** I got an email from the bank. **When** I was listening to music, I got an email from the bank. He was living in France **when** a flight attendant saw him. **When** he was living in France, a flight attendant saw him.
5. Use *while* for two events of equal or similar length that happened at the same time. One clause must be written in the **past progressive**. It can be the time clause or main clause. The other clause can be in the past progressive OR simple past.	I was traveling in Europe **while** my friends were working. I was traveling in Europe **while** my friends worked. I traveled in Europe **while** my friends were working.

*Some verbs should almost always be in the simple past (and not the past progressive):

Stative verbs: *be, know, like, love*

Short action verbs: *break my leg, cut my finger, get an email, see something*

These verbs are short actions / accidental; we don't use the progressive because the progressive focuses on things that take a long time.

2 Complete the sentences with the correct form of the words in parentheses. Use the simple past or past progressive. Add a comma when necessary. Remember to use simple past for stative and short action verbs.

1. I was living in a new town when <u>*I learned about a case of check fraud.*</u>
   (I / learn about a case of check fraud)

2. First, two men knocked on all the doors in my neighborhood while _____

   _____
   (my neighbors / relax at home on Sunday)

3. The men offered to do gardening work when _____

   _____
   (my neighbors / answer their door)

4. Next, the men asked my neighbors to write checks for $50 to their company, CAS. The men

   added an "H" to the checks when _____

   _____
   (they / take the checks to the bank)

5. The two men were stealing a lot of money when

   _____

   _____
   (a bank clerk / finally become suspicious of what they / do)

6. When the clerk called the police, _____

   _____
   (the police / arrest the two men)

7. I learned about this fraud while _____

   _____
   (I / watch the news on TV)

Note: In the United States, it is sometimes possible to get cash in exchange for checks that have *cash* written on them instead of a person's name.

3 APPLY **Think about the last time you became suspicious of something a person was doing. What were you doing? What was the other person doing? Write two sentences with *while* and two sentences with *when*. Use simple past and past progressive. Use commas when necessary.**

Go to the **Pearson Practice English App** or **MyEnglishLab** for more grammar practice. Check what you learned in **MyEnglishLab**.

FINAL WRITING TASK: A Descriptive Paragraph 🔍 APPLY

In this unit, you read about different kinds of fraud: impersonation, check fraud, and identity theft.

Now you are going to *write a paragraph describing an experience with fraud that you or someone you know has had.* Use the vocabulary and grammar from the unit.

For an alternative writing topic, see page 49.

PREPARE TO WRITE: Answering Questions

Think about an experience that you or someone you know had with fraud. Answer the questions.

1. What happened? _____

   _____

2. What made it a fraud? _____

   _____

3. What were the consequences? _____

   _____

4. How did you or the other person feel after this experience? Why? _____

   _____

5. When did you realize something was wrong? Who helped deal with the problem? _____

   _____

WRITE

Describing an Experience

When writing a paragraph to **describe an experience** or **tell a story**, it is important to begin with a clear **topic sentence** that tells **what kind of experience** it was. The **sentences that follow** tell **what happened**. They include details that support the idea of the topic sentence. The **concluding sentence** tells **what happened at the end**. Look at these examples:

- **Topic sentence:**

  When I was a college student, my identity was stolen, and it almost ruined my life.

- **What happened first:**

  I got a credit alert from my bank saying that I was over $200,000 in debt.

- **What happened next:**

  I learned that someone had opened credit cards in my name.

- **What happened next:**

  I almost had to drop out of college because I couldn't afford tuition anymore.

- **Concluding sentence:**

  The man who stole my identity was caught and my debt was cleared.

1 Read the paragraph and answer the questions.

> When my friend Jay went to a car repair shop, he had the worst experience of his life. Jay went there for a simple oil change. He was getting ready to go on a 200-mile trip to Boston, and he wanted to be sure his car was in good shape. While the mechanic was checking his engine, he said the car needed much more than an oil change. He told Jay that it needed $1,000 worth of other repairs. Jay decided to let him do all the repairs because he was concerned about his trip. The mechanic charged him a total of $1,200 when he was finished with everything. A few hours later, my friend's car suddenly broke down while he was driving to Boston. He went to another car repair service, and they told him that his engine was now broken because of the other mechanic. Jay had to pay $1,500 for more repairs. Now he had no more money left for his trip to Boston. He was very angry, so he decided to return to the first mechanic and ask for his money back. When he arrived at the car shop, it was closed. The mechanic had moved to another town, and Jay never saw him again.

1. What is the topic sentence of this paragraph?

2. How does the writer support the topic sentence?

2 Discuss your answers to the questions. Be sure to use the correct past verb forms.

1. What kind of experience is described in Exercise One? What idea is expressed in the topic sentence?

2. How do the sentences that follow support this idea? Do they include positive or negative details?

3. What happened at the end? How is the concluding sentence related to the topic sentence?

3 Look at your answers from Prepare to Write on page 44. Write a sentence describing the experience. This will be the topic sentence of your paragraph.

Example

My brother had a very embarrassing experience with a co-worker who tried to con him.

4 Write the first draft of your paragraph.

- Describe what happened and include only details that support your topic sentence.

- Write a concluding sentence that tells what happened at the end.

- Use the simple past and past progressive to show differences in time duration, interruption, and length.

REVISE: Using Topic Sentences

1 Read the paragraph. Underline the sentence that explains the main idea.

My sister wasted a lot of money when she bought a fraudulent weight loss product. She saw an ad on TV for a special kind of tea. The ad promised that people who drink the tea lose weight very quickly. While she was ordering the tea, she learned that she had to buy a six-month supply of the tea. This cost her $200. Unfortunately, the tea tasted terrible, and it made her sick. She wasted $200 on a product that didn't help her lose weight at all.

Topic Sentences

A paragraph telling a story needs to have one main idea. This main idea is expressed in the topic sentence, which is usually the first sentence. **A good topic sentence is clear.** It helps the reader to **focus on the main idea, which is supported by all the other sentences in the paragraph.**

Look at the underlined topic sentence in this paragraph. Pay attention to how the other sentences support the main idea.

I had a bad experience with a dentist who promised to make my teeth look white. First, he charged me $800 for a tooth-whitening treatment. While I was paying for the treatment, he told me that I couldn't drink coffee anymore. I stopped drinking coffee for two days, and then I wanted to start drinking it again. As soon as I drank coffee, my teeth lost their new, white look. I wish he had told me about the coffee rule before I got the treatment. This was a very bad experience for me, and I'm still angry about it.

2 Choose the best topic sentence for each paragraph.

1. _____ She was looking for a job, and she found a website for people who work at home. The website said she could make $8,000 a month running a home business. She sent an email to the manager of the website. He told her to send him a check for $100 for special training software. She sent him the check but never heard from him again. When she looked for the website again, it was gone.

   a. My friend wanted to make $8,000 a month.

   b. My friend was conned by a stranger on the internet.

   c. My friend was angry because she was cheated.

2. _____ It started when I left a magazine at the gym. It had my name and address on it. Somebody found the magazine and used my name and address to open a credit card. Soon, I started receiving bills for new clothes, furniture, and a trip to Hawaii. My bank didn't help me. My credit was ruined. I couldn't sleep or eat, and I nearly lost my job because of the terrible stress.

   a. I experienced identity theft at the gym.

   b. I had a terrible experience because of a magazine.

   c. My experience with identity theft almost destroyed my life.

3. _____ She had terrible back pain, and he told her that she needed to change her bed. He offered her a special deal on a new bed, and she bought it. When her back pain continued, he told her that she didn't need the bed at all. She needed to buy some vitamins from him. He told her to take two vitamins a day during the week and three vitamins a day on weekends. She didn't understand his advice at all because he kept telling her different things.

   a. My sister was confused by the advice of a fraudulent doctor.

   b. My sister was angry because of the advice of a fraudulent doctor.

   c. My sister still had back pain after seeing a fraudulent doctor.

3 The topic sentences in these paragraphs are not clear. They do not help the reader to focus on the main idea. Read each paragraph. Then rewrite the topic sentence to make it clear and focused.

1. Once I bought some new face cream. I wanted to look younger, and I thought the face cream would help me. But I couldn't find it anywhere. I tried four different stores in my city. Finally, I drove to another city. I got stuck in traffic for almost two hours. When I finally arrived at the store, it was closed. I went back the next week and bought the face cream. But it didn't work at all!

   New topic sentence: _____

2. We are all human, and we all make mistakes. Last year, I used a credit card to buy some language learning CDs. The sales clerk promised that I could learn three different languages while I was sleeping. Unfortunately, I learned nothing. I tried to return the CDs, but I couldn't get my money back. It took me several months to pay for them, and I really regret buying the CDs.

   New topic sentence: _____

3. My uncle is really nice but doesn't always make the best decisions. He has been bald for a long time. Last year, he saw an ad for a new hair product on TV. He bought the product and used it right away. Then he went to a party and noticed that people were laughing at him. He looked in a mirror and saw that his bald head was turning blue. He tried washing off the color, but nothing worked.

New topic sentence: _____

4 Now go back to the first draft of your paragraph.

- Make sure your topic sentence is clear and focused and that the rest of the information in your paragraph supports it.

- Try to use the grammar and some of the vocabulary from the unit.

⊙ Go to **MyEnglishLab** for more skill practice.

EDIT: Writing the Final Draft

APPLY Write the final draft of your paragraph and submit it to your teacher. Carefully edit it for grammatical and mechanical errors, such as spelling, capitalization, and punctuation. Consider how to apply the vocabulary, grammar, and writing skills from the unit. Use the checklist to help you.

FINAL DRAFT CHECKLIST

☐ Is your topic sentence clear and focused?

☐ Are all the supporting details related to the topic sentence?

☐ Does your paragraph clearly describe what happened in the experience?

☐ Does the concluding sentence explain what happened at the end?

☐ Are the simple past and past progressive verbs used correctly?

☐ Is your paragraph formatted correctly?

☐ Do you use new vocabulary from the unit?

ALTERNATIVE WRITING TOPIC

APPLY In this unit you read about different types of fraud. Write a paragraph describing examples of how technology has increased both the types of fraud and the frequency with which it occurs. Use the grammar and vocabulary from the unit.

CHECK WHAT YOU'VE LEARNED

Check (✔) the outcomes you've met and vocabulary you've learned. Put an X next to the skills and vocabulary you still need to practice.

Learning Outcomes

☐ **Infer comparisons**

☐ **Take notes with questions**

☐ **Identify detailed examples**

☐ **Use simple past and past progressive**

☐ **Use topic sentences**

☐ **Write a descriptive paragraph**

Vocabulary

☐ astonishing

☐ con (*v.*)

☐ convincing (*adj.*) AWL

☐ deception

☐ duplicate

☐ fake (*adj.*)

☐ fishy

☐ fraud

☐ honesty

☐ impersonate

☐ impress

☐ motive AWL

☐ suspicious

☐ weary

 Go to **MyEnglishLab** to watch a video about identity theft, access the Unit Project, and take the Unit 2 Achievement Test.

LEARNING OUTCOMES

> Infer degrees of difficulty
> Mark a text
> Scan for details

> Use infinitives of purpose
> Use parallel structure
> Write a pro and con paragraph

Go to **MyEnglishLab** to check what you know.

Exploring the Red Planet

1 FOCUS ON THE TOPIC

1. Exploring space costs a tremendous amount of money. Do you think what is learned from space exploration is worth the cost?

2. What do you know about Mars? How have scientists learned about Mars in the past? What do scientists hope to learn in the future?

READING ONE | Mars: Our New Home?

VOCABULARY

1 Read the article about a family living on Mars time. Pay attention to the boldfaced words.

ONE FAMILY'S "VACATION" TO MARS

When the Curiosity rover[1] landed on Mars in August of 2012, many of the mission's scientists on Earth decided to live on Mars time for the first 90 days of the mission. They had learned from earlier Mars missions that it is upsetting to their ability to sleep well when they are on Earth time at home and on Mars time at work. And they know that lack of sleep can lead to **depression**. Such stress does not allow them to keep working. In addition, by changing their schedules to Mars time and **simulating** Martian days on Earth, they were able to control the actions of Curiosity when the rover was facing Earth. The Earth takes 24 hours to **spin** around once, but Mars

Curiosity exploring Mars

takes 24 hours and 40 minutes. Mars time quickly becomes different from an Earth day. For example, in two-and-a-half weeks, noon on Mars becomes 4:00 A.M. on Earth. The NASA scientists knew it would be a challenge to live and work on Mars time for 90 days. In fact, some of them didn't succeed in making the difficult change in their schedules. They had to go back to a normal Earth schedule due to the difficulties that an additional 40 minutes brought to their daily routine. Those scientists that didn't **survive** the 90 days said they felt **isolated** from their families because they rarely saw them.

David Oh, the Curiosity mission's head scientist, knew being separated from his family would be difficult for him. He knew that he would miss them very much even though they would be living in the same house. He was **counting on** three months of loneliness, but his family surprised him. For a month before school started, his wife and three children lived on Mars time with him. At first, he and his family thought that they would have a month of **boredom** because there would be nothing to do. Their **artificial** 24-hour-and-40-minute day would not offer a lot of activities for a young family of five. But soon they found a lot to do: bowling, eating at all-night diners, walking on the beach in moonlight, and seeing meteors[2] when the moon was not bright. They also cooked together, ate together, and watched movies together. David and his wife Bryn were most surprised by their children's **reaction**: they loved it and want to have another "vacation" to Mars during their next break from school!

---

[1] **rover:** a vehicle for exploring the surface of a moon or planet
[2] **meteor:** a small piece of rock that produces a bright line in the sky when it falls from space

2 **Match the words on the left with the definitions on the right.**

_____ 1. depression   a. feeling alone and unable to meet or speak to other people

_____ 2. simulate   b. to make something look, sound, or feel like something else

_____ 3. spin   c. to expect something to be true

_____ 4. survive   d. to turn around and around

_____ 5. isolated   e. tired and impatient because you have nothing to do

_____ 6. count on   f. not real or natural, but made by people

_____ 7. boredom   g. something that you feel or do because of something that has
                               happened or been said

_____ 8. artificial   h. to continue to live normally in spite of dangers and difficulties

_____ 9. reaction   i. being so sad and upset that you are unable to do anything

Go to the **Pearson Practice English App** or **MyEnglishLab** for more vocabulary practice.

PREVIEW

Look at the title of the reading and the photo. Make a list of questions that you think will be answered in this reading.

1. _____

2. _____

3. _____

READ

Read the article about Mars on the next page. Create a chart like the one below to take notes. On the left, put the main ideas. On the right, put the details.

TAKE NOTES

Main Ideas	Details
Mars One — looking for colonists	Dutch Co. need skills

Go to **MyEnglishLab** to view example notes.

MARS: OUR NEW HOME?

a design for a colony on Mars

1 If you think you'd like to live on Mars, you may have that possibility by 2031. A Dutch company called Mars One is looking for people interested in colonizing[1] Mars. If you have all the necessary skills— and there are a lot—you could be one of the first colonists to Mars. Are you ready for the challenge?

2 Luckily, you won't have to find the money to pay for a mission to Mars because it would cost billions of dollars. Mars One has already received money from companies and some private donors[2]. It is also **counting on** getting money from everyday people who become interested in the Mars One TV show. On this show, colonists will be selected as people around the world watch. The show will follow teams of four applicants as they complete difficult jobs in difficult situations. The audience will vote for the best six teams. The show will be seen worldwide both on television and online. Mars One is hoping that people will become so interested in the mission that they will give large and small amounts of money . . . or at least buy a T-shirt or coffee mug—which are already available on Mars One's website.

3 As a future colonist in one of the six teams, you will go through years of training. If your team is the first team to travel to Mars, your main responsibility when you get there will be to build a place where humans can live. The atmosphere on Mars does not have enough oxygen[3] for humans, and the land is not good enough to grow food. Colonists will have to create an **artificial** environment on Mars where there is air to breathe and land to farm. Scientists know Earth-like conditions can be **simulated** on Mars because something similar has already been done in Antarctica, where humans cannot **survive** outside the created environment.

4 Humans may have another problem in space as well. It takes nearly a year to get to Mars, so travelers would be without the Earth's gravity[4] for a long time. In addition, Mars One astronauts will not return to Earth. Their mission is to start a colony that can support itself. So, the colonists will live the rest of their lives there. When a human lives in an environment without gravity or with low gravity[5] for a long time, the systems in the body weaken. For example, muscles and bones lose strength. The heart also gets weaker. The blood in the body gets thicker, and it becomes more difficult for the heart to push blood through the body. In space, **spinning** the spaceship can create artificial gravity which can help these problems. On Mars, colonists would need to exercise and take medications to stay healthy.

5 It will also be difficult for Mars colonists to be **isolated**, far from home, living in small spaces, and seeing the same people over and over. It is important to come up with solutions to possible problems before anyone actually goes on a Mars mission. For instance, Mars One could make plans for colonists to communicate with friends and family on Earth. Also, people interested in the mission could be evaluated to make sure they have the emotional strength to survive. Colonists with **depression** could put the mission in danger. Fortunately, a few years ago, a joint Russian and European project called the Mars500 Mission took place. It studied people's **reactions** to long-term space travel by following six astronauts in a Mars-like environment. The astronauts spent 520 days in this environment and only had contact with their bosses and their families. The six astronauts "returned" to Earth in good physical condition—and they were still speaking nicely to each other, which is astonishing when you think about their difficult experience. Scientists viewed the Mars500 Mission as a great success because they were able to see how the astronauts handle emotional and physical stresses. Surprisingly, the greatest emotional problem was **boredom**. The greatest physical problems were not getting enough sleep and gaining too much weight.

6 Recent polls show that 7 percent of people would want to go on such an adventure. Mars One has already started accepting applications for colonists. Applicants do not have to have any specific training, but they must be interested in learning new things and capable of solving problems. They also should be able to trust others and complete an assignment without stopping. Interested?

---

[1] **colonize:** to control an area and send your own people there to live
[2] **donor:** someone who gives something, especially money, to an organization
[3] **oxygen:** a gas in the air that has no color, smell, or taste. People, animals, and plants need it to live.
[4] **gravity:** Earth's gravity is what keeps you on the ground and what causes things to fall
[5] **low gravity:** the gravity on Mars is only 38 percent of Earth's gravity

MAIN IDEAS

Read the statements and check (✓) the four main ideas. Use your notes to help you. Compare the main ideas to your notes and put the number of the paragraph next to the letter.

☐ _____ a. Colonists could experience feelings of isolation, depression, and boredom.

☐ _____ b. Mars One has already started accepting applications for colonists.

☐ _____ c. Colonists will have to make Mars a place where they can live.

☐ _____ d. A TV show will help raise money for the mission.

☐ _____ e. Mars One has a website that sells products.

☐ _____ f. The human body needs gravity to stay strong.

DETAILS

1 Choose the correct answer. Use your notes to help you.

1. Which step is NOT part of the application process?

   a. Choose your team of four.

   b. Participate in challenging activities.

   c. Be on worldwide television.

2. How many teams of colonists will be trained to go to Mars?

   a. four

   b. five

   c. six

3. What body parts get weaker in lower gravity?

   a. brain

   b. bones

   c. lungs

4. When the Mars500 astronauts returned to Earth, they were _____ .

   a. angry at each other

   b. heavier than they were before they left

   c. bored and tired

5. What can colonists expect when they move to Mars?

   a. to be without Earth's gravity

   b. to have an emotional breakdown

   c. to pay a lot of money for the trip

2 Look at your notes and at your answers in Preview. How did they help you understand the article?

Inferring Degrees of Difficulty

An **inference** is an **educated guess** about something that is **not directly stated** in a text. Writers sometimes **suggest degrees of difficulty** without stating them explicitly. A strong reader can **infer** these **degrees of difficulty** by reading the text closely.

Look at the example and read the explanation.

Considering the cost, how difficult will it be for people to join the mission to Mars?

Choose the best answer. Write an *X* on the best place on the scale.

Very easy ————————————————————————————————— Very difficult
          1   **2**   **3**   **4**   **5**

(The best answer is toward the left side / easy.)

In **paragraph 2,** we learn that colonists will not have to pay for their trip. Companies and private donors will supply the money for this mission. There may be other financial implications, including having to give up your job, for example.

After reading the text closely, we can **infer** that, in terms of cost, joining the mission **won't be so difficult** since people won't have to pay anything.

1 **Choose the best answer for each challenge the colonists will face on the Mars mission. Look at the paragraphs in parentheses.**

1. How difficult will it be to create an artificial environment? *(paragraph 3)*

Very easy ————————————————————————————————— Very difficult
          1   2   3   4   5

2. How difficult will it be to live without or with low gravity? *(paragraph 4)*

Very easy ————————————————————————————————— Very difficult
          1   2   3   4   5

3. How difficult will it be to deal with feelings of isolation? *(paragraph 5)*

Very easy ————————————————————————————————— Very difficult
          1   2   3   4   5

4. How difficult will it be to prevent boredom? *(paragraph 5)*

Very easy ————————————————————————————————— Very difficult
          1   2   3   4   5

2 **Now discuss your answers with a partner. Point out words, phrases, or statements in the paragraphs that helped you find the answers.**

DISCUSS 🔍

Work in small groups. Choose one of the questions. Discuss your ideas. Then choose one person in your group to report the ideas to the class.

USE YOUR NOTES

Use your notes to support your answers with information from the reading.

1. Scientists believe that the information they learned from the Mars 500 project was valuable in understanding what colonists to Mars might have to face. Do you agree? Why or why not?

2. Mars One is a very complex project. What kinds of problems will make it difficult? What kinds of people, in terms of professions or areas of expertise, will be critical to the project?

3. What kinds of emotional or physical issues might the colonists have? Will these issues be difficult to deal with? Why or why not?

➤ Go to **MyEnglishLab** to give your opinion about another question.

READING TWO | Timeline for a Mission to Mars

PREVIEW

1 Look at the title and the photo below. Read the first paragraph. Write two questions that you think will be answered in this reading.

_____

_____

2 Look at the boldfaced words in the reading. Which words do you know the meaning of?

READ

1 Read the online article about a timeline for going to Mars. As you read, guess the meanings of the words that are new to you. Remember to take notes on main ideas and details.

Timeline for a Mission to Mars

NASA currently has five spaceships orbiting[1] Mars and one rover on the planet, but they don't have plans to send colonists there like Mars One does. Sending anyone to Mars—colonists for the rest of their lives or astronauts for two months—takes a lot of planning. Space researchers have suggested plans for sending people to Mars, and their plans are based on real facts. But since no one has ever gone to Mars, their plans are only **speculations**. For example, the people at Discovery Channel made a movie called *Race to Mars*, which follows a realistic timeline. The magazine *Popular Science* has also written about the steps needed to go to Mars. What kinds of events might scientists agree on? Here is a plan that might be proposed.

An artist's drawing of the Mars Reconnaissance Orbiter, which is studying Mars

Days 1–97	**Launching[2] Spaceships** Parts for the three supply ships and one passenger ship are launched and begin to orbit the Earth. Spaceship builders put the ships together. After that, the three supply ships leave for Mars. The passenger ship waits in orbit until the astronauts arrive.
Days 98–112	**Checking the Health of the Astronauts** The astronauts stay away from other people for two weeks before leaving Earth to avoid getting sick. Doctors make sure they are in good health.
Days 113–115	**Launching the Astronauts** The astronauts leave Earth in the fifth ship and meet the passenger ship already in orbit. The ship connects to the passenger ship. The astronauts enter the passenger ship and make sure everything is in good working order.
Day 116	**Leaving Earth** The **engines** fire to help the passenger ship leave the Earth's gravity. When the ship is in space, it begins to spin around. The spinning creates artificial gravity.

---

[1] **orbit:** to move around a planet such as the Earth while in space
[2] **launch:** to send a spaceship into the sky or into space

Continued on next page

Days 116–356   **Traveling to Mars**
The trip to Mars takes 240 days. The schedule for each day is similar to a typical Earth day. *(See Daily Schedule for Trip to Mars)*

Day 342   **Reaching Mars: Supply Ships**
The supply ships arrive almost two weeks before the passenger ship does. After these ships are in orbit around Mars, two of the ships land on the surface. Because they were programmed on Earth, the ships begin to work **automatically**. One of the supply ships is the artificial habitat, and it needs to be **established** in an appropriate area. The area needs to be large enough for the astronauts to do their **research** and prepare their experiments. The third supply ship waits in orbit for the passenger ship to arrive.

Day 356   **Reaching Mars: Passenger Ship**
After the passenger ship stops spinning, it enters orbit around Mars. It connects to the third supply ship. Then the astronauts land on Mars. The passenger ship stays in orbit.

Day 357   **Beginning Mission**
The astronauts move into the artificial habitat, which supplies oxygen but not full gravity. They begin their exploration of Mars, which includes drilling for water, collecting rocks, and doing experiments to determine if there was ever life on Mars.

Day 417   **Leaving Mars**
The astronauts take off from Mars and connect to the passenger ship. They check the ship, get it ready, and begin their return to Earth.

Day 657   **Landing on Earth**
The astronauts get into the small ship and land on Earth in the ocean.

Daily Schedule for Trip to Mars	
07:00	Artificial light comes on slowly to simulate sunrise
07:30	Breakfast
08:00–12:00	Work period (maintaining ship's systems)
12:15	Lunch
12:45–14:30	Free time (exercise, read, contact people on Earth, practice hobbies)
14:30–17:30	Work period
17:30–18:30	Exercise period
18:45	Dinner
19:30–22:00	Free time
22:30	Artificial light turns off slowly to simulate sunset
23:00	Lights out

2 Compare your notes on main ideas and details with a partner's. How can you improve your notes next time?

Go to the **Pearson Practice English App** or **My**English**Lab** for more vocabulary practice.

Marking a Text

When you mark a text, you identify important information. This helps you read more carefully. You can look back at the information you marked to help you study for tests and complete assignments.

There are several ways to mark a text.

Underline	<u>Draw a line under</u> the information.
Circle	Circle the information.
Highlight	Highlight the information with a colored highlighter pen.

Only mark the important information you want to find later. For example, these marks focus on the types of missions NASA has on Mars:

> NASA currently has five spaceships orbiting Mars and one rover on the planet, but they don't have plans to send colonists there like Mars One does.

Don't mark too much information. If you mark too much information, you will not be able to find the important information later.

> NASA currently has five spaceships orbiting Mars and one rover on the planet, but they don't have plans to send colonists there like Mars One does.

1 **Find the information in the text that helps you answer the questions. Choose a method to mark the text. Share your answers with a partner.**

a. Who will pay for the Mars One mission?

> Luckily, you won't have to find the money to pay for a mission to Mars because it would cost billions of dollars. Mars One has already received money from companies and some private donors. It is also counting on getting money from everyday people who become interested in the Mars One TV show.

b. What will the first colonists need to do on Mars?

> As a future colonist in one of the six teams, you will go through years of training. If your team is the first team to travel to Mars, your main responsibility when you get there will be to build a place where humans can live. The atmosphere on Mars does not have enough oxygen for humans, and the land is not good enough to grow food. Colonists will have to create an artificial environment on Mars where there is air to breathe and land to farm.

2 **Look at Reading Two again. Mark the information you think is the most important.**

Go to **MyEnglishLab** for more note-taking practice.

COMPREHENSION

1 Answer the questions. Use your notes from Reading Two to help you. Discuss your answers with a partner.

1. According to the proposed timeline, how long would it take to reach Mars, complete the mission, and return to Earth?

2. Five spaceships are used for the mission. What is the purpose of each ship?

3. How do the astronauts survive on Mars with no oxygen?

4. How many work hours are there in the daily schedule during the trip to Mars?

2 Review the boldfaced words from the reading with a partner. Use a dictionary or ask your teacher for any meanings you still do not know.

READING SKILL

1 Look at Reading Two again. When you looked for the boldfaced words in Preview, did you read quickly or carefully? Why did you read the way you did?

Scanning for Details

Scanning allows you to **find information quickly** without having to read the entire text. Before you read Reading Two, you were asked to look at the boldfaced words. That was scanning.

In addition to **boldfaced words,** you can scan for **key words, names, numbers, places,** and **dates.** Key words are words that are often repeated. Look for capital letters when you want to find a name. Numbers are easy to find.

Scanning is very useful when taking tests with a reading. First read the questions, and then scan the reading for the answers.

When you find specific information by scanning, you can mark it in the text by underlining, circling, or highlighting the information so that you can find it again later. You can also add the scanned information as details to your notes.

Examples:

Question: Who made the movie *Race to Mars?*

Answer: The Discovery Channel

(SCAN: Find the title of the movie in italics and read around it. MARK: Underline or circle the title.)

Question: What happens on Day 417?

Answer: The astronauts leave Mars.

(SCAN: Find that number on the list and just read what happens that day. MARK: Underline the key words.)

2 **Work with a partner. Scan Reading Two for answers to the questions. When you find an answer, mark it in the text. The information in parentheses tells you where to scan.**

1. How many NASA rovers are on Mars? How many ships orbit the planet? *(paragraph 1)*

2. What do astronauts do during their free time? *(daily schedule)*

3. What do the astronauts do between 17:30–18:30? *(daily schedule)*

4. What is created when the spaceship spins around? *(Day 116)*

5. The artificial habitat supplies something important for life. What is it? *(Day 357)*

Go to **MyEnglishLab** for more skill practice.

CONNECT THE READINGS 🔍

ORGANIZE

Reading One (R1) and Reading Two (R2) contain information about Mars missions. Complete the chart with information from the readings.

PROBLEM	SOLUTION
1. No oxygen in Mars atmosphere	
2. Low gravity → weak muscles, bones, and heart	
3. Feel isolated → far from home	
4. Boredom	Keep busy → don't get bored
5.	Keep busy → feel tired, sleep better
6.	Required exercise periods

SYNTHESIZE

Work with a partner. Complete the sentences with information from the chart.

There are several problems we must solve before people can live on Mars. The first problem is that people cannot live in the environment on Mars. For example, _____ . In addition, _____ . The solution to this problem is _____ .

Another problem is psychological. Colonists may feel _____ _____ and experience _____ _____ . To solve these problems, colonists can _____ . They can also _____ .

Finally, the colonists on Mars may have physical problems, such as _____ _____ or _____ _____ . They can avoid these problems if they _____ _____ and _____ _____ . This will help them _____ _____ .

Go to **My**English**Lab** to check what you learned.

VOCABULARY

REVIEW

Complete the crossword puzzle. Read the clues and choose words from the box.

artificial	depression	isolated	simulate	spin
automatically	engines	reaction	speculation	survive
boredom	establish	research		

Across

2. Small cells deep in the rock on Mars have been found, but they must be _____ from the rock in order to study them.

5. When there is a problem with Curiosity, a message is _____ sent to Earth.

8. There has been _____ about life on Mars for a long time.

9. For any living thing to _____ on Mars, there needs to be water.

10. Mars One will develop habitats on Mars that _____ the habitats in Antarctica.

13. As in previous Mars missions, scientists _____ the rovers to collect rocks.

Down

1. What would your _____ be if life were discovered on Mars?

3. Without enough sleep, the astronauts may develop _____ .

4. Without _____ , rovers cannot move around on the surface of Mars.

6. _____ suggests that life on Mars may have been possible thousands of years ago.

7. _____ isn't a problem if you are studying the possibility of life on Mars.

10. Planets _____ around much more slowly than spaceships do.

11. _____ habitats must be built on Mars in order for colonists to live there.

12. Scientists hope to _____ a Mars base in the future.

EXPAND

1 Complete the sentences with one of the words from the box. The missing word and the boldfaced word make up a common expression.

artificial	automatic	establish	isolated	simulator

1. _____ **intelligence** is the science that allows computers to think and make decisions.

2. A **flight** _____ is a machine that makes you feel like you are flying, but you're really on the ground. It is used for training.

3. An _____ **incident** is an event that usually does not happen often or that happened only once.

4. An _____ **pilot** system allows airplanes to fly themselves.

5. To _____ **yourself** is to do something that makes people notice you and take your skills seriously.

2 Write the five expressions. You will need them for the next activity.

_____   _____

_____   _____

_____

CREATE

APPLY **Complete the journal entry by one of the future Mars colonists. Use three of the expressions from Expand and at least five new words from this unit.**

Year 3, Day 1

I am just starting my third year of training to be a colonist on Mars, and I am really tired. Sometimes, I don't know why I wanted to do this.

_____

_____

_____

_____

_____

But, when I think about everything, _____

_____

_____

_____

_____

Lights out! I must go to bed now.

Go to the **Pearson Practice English App** or **MyEnglishLab** for more vocabulary practice.

GRAMMAR FOR WRITING

1 **Read the sentences. Underline the verbs that have the form *to* + verb. What questions do these verbs answer?**

- The engines fire to leave orbit.
- The mission was started to build a colony.
- The ship is spinning to create artificial gravity.

Infinitives of Purpose

Questions	Answers
Why do the engines fire?	They fire **to leave** Earth's orbit.
Why was the mission started?	It was started **to build** a colony on Mars.
Why is the ship spinning?	It is spinning **to create** artificial gravity.
1. Infinitives (**to** + **verb**) that are used to explain the purpose of an action are called **infinitives of purpose**. They answer the question **Why**?	The engines fire **to leave** Earth's orbit. The mission was started **to build** a colony on Mars. The ship is spinning **to create** artificial gravity.
2. You can also use the longer form **in order to** + **verb**.	The engines fire **in order to leave** Earth's orbit. The mission was started **in order to build** a colony on Mars. The ship is spinning **in order to create** artificial gravity.
3. Use **in order not to** + verb to express a negative purpose.	The ship is spinning **in order not to** cause bones and muscles to weaken.

2 Match the questions on the left with the answers on the right.

Questions	Answers
_____ 1. Why does Mars One need money?	a. in order not to get sick
_____ 2. Why do the colonists use the radio?	b. to go to Mars
_____ 3. Why are the astronauts isolated before leaving on a trip to Mars?	c. in order to talk to their families on Earth
_____ 4. Why does Mars One have a selection committee?	d. to strengthen muscles and bones
_____ 5. Why will colonists exercise a lot?	e. to choose four astronauts

3 Combine the questions and answers from Exercise Two to make sentences that answer the question "Why?"

1. _Mars One needs money to go to Mars._ _____

2. _____

3. _____

4. _____

5. _____

Go to the **Pearson Practice English App** or **MyEnglishLab** for more grammar practice. Check what you learned in **MyEnglishLab**.

In this unit, you read about a plan to build a colony on Mars. The job of a colonist is open to anyone. What are the pros and cons of accepting this position? Would you go on a Mars mission? Why or why not?

You are going to *write a paragraph answering this question and giving reasons for your decision*.

What are the pros and cons of deciding one way or the other? Evaluate your own abilities.

For an alternative writing topic, see page 73.

PREPARE TO WRITE: Evaluating Pros and Cons

Complete the chart with the pros and cons of going to Mars. Don't think too much. Quickly list any ideas that come to mind.

PROS	CONS

WRITE

Creating a Paragraph Outline

An **outline** is a plan for how you will write a text. The outline here is an example of a **paragraph outline**. An outline will help you to organize the main idea and details that you want to include, as well as your topic sentence, supporting points, supporting details, and concluding sentence.

> **I.** Topic Sentence
>
> **II.** Supporting Point
>
>   **A.** Supporting Detail
>
>   **B.** Supporting Detail
>
> **III.** Supporting Point
>
>   **A.** Supporting Detail
>
>   **B.** Supporting Detail
>
> **IV.** Supporting Point
>
>   **A.** Supporting Detail
>
>   **B.** Supporting Detail
>
> **V.** Concluding Sentence

1 Read the paragraph about a difficult decision. Then discuss the questions with a partner.

WHY PEOPLE JOIN MARS ONE

After graduating, some very **accomplished** students choose to apply to Mars One instead of working for a company or university. Why would someone make this choice? One reason is the **unthinkable challenge** of going into space without a chance to return. Some people like this kind of **challenge** because they want to avoid the **boredom** of an ordinary life. Secondly, these men and women want to travel in space in order to learn more about our **astonishing** universe. Perhaps they would see amazing things like asteroids and stars on the way. The last reason is to enjoy the excitement of going to a completely new place where no humans have ever gone before. This is a very **risky** decision. Although the choice to join Mars One is difficult, many people believe that developing a community on Mars is a critical way for humans to **survive**, as well as being the adventure of a lifetime.

1. What choice did the writer face?

2. How many reasons did the writer give for the decision?

3. What were the reasons? State each reason using an infinitive of purpose.

2 Complete the outline with information from the paragraph.

    I. Topic Sentence: _After graduating, some very accomplished students choose to apply to Mars One instead of working for a company or university._

  II. Supporting Point (Reason #1): _the unthinkable challenge of going into space_
     Supporting Details: _to avoid the boredom of an ordinary life_

 III. Supporting Point (Reason #2): _____
     Supporting Details: _____

 IV. Supporting Point (Reason #3): _____
     Supporting Details: _____

3 Look at your chart from Prepare to Write on page 68. Organize your ideas into an outline. Use your outline to write the first draft of your paragraph.

- Make sure you have a strong **topic sentence**.

- Include **two or three supporting points**. Each one should focus on the reasons for your opinion. Use an infinitive of purpose for each reason. Include details to explain each supporting point.

- Write a **concluding sentence** that summarizes your reasons.

REVISE: Using Parallel Structure

1 Read the sentences about jobs at NASA. Label the subjects and the verbs.

- Most people think you have to have an advanced degree to work at NASA, but many jobs do not require engineering or science degrees.

- NASA has locations in California, Texas, Louisiana, Florida, and Maryland.

Parallel Structure

Writers use **parallel structure** when writing sentences with two or three words or phrases of the same part of speech (noun, verb, adjective, adverb), allowing them to express several ideas in one sentence.

- NASA employees **plan space missions, study weather patterns, fix computers,** and **type letters**.

- NASA is looking for **intelligent and educated** college graduates to work for them.

Two ideas can be expressed in one sentence:

- When I went online, I **found** the NASA job openings.

- When I went online, I **read** about the types of jobs I could do.

- When I went online, I **found** the NASA job openings and **read** about the types of jobs I could do.

A third idea can be added:

- When I went online, I **applied** for a job.

- When I went online, I **found** the NASA job openings, **read** about the types of jobs I could do, and **applied** for a job.
  *(Notice that **found, read,** and **applied** are all in the past form.)*

Look at two more examples:

    [ADV] [V]   [ADV]   [V]
- I **easily filled** out the application and **successfully submitted** it.
(The phrases are parallel because they both contain an adverb and a verb.)

         [ADJ]   [N]   [ADJ]   [N]
- I hope the job has a **good environment** and **friendly colleagues**.
(The phrases are parallel because they both contain an adjective and a noun.)

2 Combine each pair of sentences using parallel structure.

1. NASA treats its employees well.

   NASA pays its employees well.

   _____

   _____

2. NASA carefully reviews each candidate.

   NASA fairly reviews each candidate.

   _____

   _____

3. In college, I studied astronomy.

   In college, I studied geology.

   _____

   _____

4. On my first day at my new job, the boss was very helpful.

   On my first day at my new job, my co-workers were very helpful.

   _____

   _____

5. When the Curiosity rover landed on Mars, I went on Mars time.

   When the Curiosity rover landed on Mars, I didn't see my family very much.

   _____

   _____

6. NASA has safely launched many spaceships.

   NASA has proudly launched many spaceships.

   _____

   _____

7. I learned a lot during my first year at NASA.

   I made many friends during my first year at NASA.

   _____

   _____

3 Describe the dream job of people who are interested in space. Complete the paragraph. Use parallel structure.

> ## Jobs in Space
>
> People who are interested in space would like to work there. The jobs they want are
>
> _____, _____, and _____. People
>   (ADJ)   (ADJ)   (ADJ)
>
> who get these jobs are talented because they can _____ and
>   (V)
>
> _____. Workers in space are respected because they do their jobs so
>   (V)
>
> _____ and _____. They love their jobs in space
>   (ADV)   (ADV)
>
> because of _____ _____ and _____
>   (ADJ)   (N)   (ADJ)
>
> _____ .
>   (N)

4 **Now go back to the first draft of your paragraph.**

- Rewrite at least three or four sentences using parallel structure.

- Try to use the grammar and some of the vocabulary from the unit.

▶ Go to **MyEnglishLab** for more skill practice.

EDIT: Writing the Final Draft

APPLY Write the final draft of your paragraph and submit it to your teacher. Carefully edit it for grammatical and mechanical errors, such as spelling, capitalization, and punctuation. Consider how to apply the vocabulary, grammar, pronunciation, and writing skills from the unit. Use the checklist to help you.

FINAL DRAFT CHECKLIST

☐ Does your paragraph clearly explain the reasons for your decision?

☐ Does it contain a topic sentence, two or three supporting points, and a concluding sentence?

☐ Does each supporting point focus clearly on one reason?

☐ Are there details to explain each supporting point?

☐ Does the concluding sentence summarize the supporting points (the reasons)?

☐ Are there at least three infinitives of purpose, and are they used correctly?

☐ Does your paragraph use parallel structure?

☐ Do you use new vocabulary from the unit?

ALTERNATIVE WRITING TOPIC

APPLY Mars One is privately funded, but other space programs, like those in the United States, are funded by taxpayer money. Do you think spending money on space programs is worth the money that is spent? Why or why not?

CHECK WHAT YOU'VE LEARNED

Check (✔) the outcomes you've met and vocabulary you've learned. Put an X next to the skills and vocabulary you still need to practice.

Learning Outcomes
☐ Infer degrees of difficulty
☐ Mark a text
☐ Scan for details
☐ Use infinitives of purpose
☐ Use parallel structure
☐ Write a pro and con paragraph

Vocabulary
☐ artificial
☐ automatically AWL
☐ boredom
☐ depression AWL
☐ engine
☐ establish AWL
☐ isolated (*adj.*) AWL

☐ reaction AWL
☐ research (*n.*) AWL
☐ simulate AWL
☐ speculation
☐ spin (*v.*)
☐ survive AWL

Multi-word Units
☐ count on

 Go to **MyEnglishLab** to watch a video about space, access the Unit Project, and take the Unit 3 Achievement Test.

LEARNING OUTCOMES

> Infer meanings of proverbs
> Take notes with a T-chart
> Recognize how examples support opinions

> Use comparative adverbs
> Use transitions of contrast
> Write a contrast paragraph

Go to **MyEnglishLab** to check what you know.

Language and Power

1 FOCUS ON THE TOPIC

1. What are some difficulties that you might have when trying to communicate with people from other cultures and nationalities?

2. Read the title of the unit. How do language and power relate to each other?

3. What are some ways that people use language differently depending on who they are talking to? Can you think of some ways that power affects language?

VOCABULARY

1 Read the description of a college course in linguistics, the scientific study of language and the use of language in societies. Pay attention to the boldfaced words.

Gender Differences in Language

In this course, we will study how men and women have traditionally used language differently. We will answer the following questions:

1. Communication and the ability to express ourselves to others using our words is an important part of life in every culture. Does our gender identity affect how we communicate? How do we use language to communicate who we are and which things are most **valued** in our lives?

2. Many people believe there are differences in the way that males and females use language. Is it true that men are more **assertive** than women and communicate more directly? Is it a **myth** that women use language more politely than men? Another example of gender differences is in the use of **profanity**. Some people feel uncomfortable hearing profanity from all people, while others only feel uncomfortable hearing profanity from women. Why?

3. Our home culture strongly affects our behavior. In our home culture, we learn how males and females are supposed to act. We also learn how much talking is acceptable to others and how much is considered **excessive**. One way to understand a culture is to look at its **proverbs**, including those about language and gender. What do proverbs show us about a culture's way of thinking about males and females?

4. Is it possible to know the gender of a speaker just by listening to his or her speech? What about the idea that females are more **talkative** than males or that men **dominate** more conversations? Where do these ideas come from?

5. All human beings want to be respected by others. They want others to admire them, and they want to feel important. What about **sexist** treatment of women based on the belief that they are **inferior** to men? How does this affect our thinking about language and gender?

2 Match the words on the left with the definitions on the right.

_____ 1. assertive

_____ 2. dominate

_____ 3. excessive

_____ 4. inferior

_____ 5. myth

_____ 6. profanity

_____ 7. proverb

_____ 8. sexist

_____ 9. talkative

_____ 10. valued

a. relating to the idea that people are treated unfairly because of their sex

b. honored and respected

c. weaker or less important

d. talking a lot

e. behaving in a confident way so that people notice you

f. to have power or control over

g. an idea that many people believe, though it is not true

h. very rude or disrespectful language

i. too much

j. a traditional saying that gives advice about life

🅚 Go to the **Pearson Practice English App** or **MyEnglishLab** for more vocabulary practice.

PREVIEW

You are going to read a student's essay about men, women, and language. Read the first paragraph on the next page. Then complete these stereotypes[1] with the words _men_ or _women_, based on how you think the writer will answer the questions she asks in the first paragraph.

1. _____Men_____ joke more than _____women_____ .

2. _____ speak more politely than _____ .

3. _____ complain less than _____ .

4. _____ gossip more than _____ .

5. _____ ask for directions more often than _____ .

_____

[1] **stereotype:** an idea of what a type of person is like that might be unfair or untrue

READ

Read the essay about men, women, and language on the next page. Create a chart like the one below to take notes. On the left, put the main ideas. On the right, put the details.

TAKE NOTES

Main Ideas	Details
Gender	Differences in male / female behavior, including language use
Differences in male / female language = differences in power	

🅚 Go to **MyEnglishLab** to view example notes.

MEN, WOMEN, and LANGUAGE

1 Imagine a playground in the United States. A boy, Ashton, and a girl, Laney, are playing with other children. Will their games be the same? What about the ways they talk to each other? Will their use of language be the same? It's difficult to answer these questions without thinking about gender, the differences that we can see in the behavior of males and females in various cultures. This behavior includes language use, the way that males and females use their words to communicate with others and to express themselves.

2 Are these differences really based on how we naturally communicate as males or females? Or do the differences come from our culture? Ideas about male and female communication have differed greatly throughout time and across different cultures. Despite these different ways of thinking, however, we can see a connection between women's power and how their communication is seen by others. As women gain more power through education and employment, they begin to use language in more **assertive** ways. In many countries around the world, the power of women has increased in the past hundred years. It is possible that this increase in power may have an effect on communication, and we may soon discover that men and women have more similarities than differences in how they communicate.

Gender and Communication: Distant Past

3 Historically, men have held positions of power more frequently than women in many cultures. This has created differences in how women and men communicate and how their words are valued. These differences have existed throughout history. One way to examine cultural views on language and see how these ideas have been a part of human history is to look at ancient **proverbs** considering the place of women in society. For centuries, people around the world have said that women are too **talkative**. We can see this idea in several proverbs, including these:

> "A woman's tongue is her weapon[1], and she does not let it rust[2]." (Chinese)

> "It's an unhappy house where the hen[3] is louder than the rooster[4]." (French)

> "A woman's hair is long, but her tongue is even longer." (Russian)

4 These proverbs show us the view of women in past times, when a woman's speech was not seen as very important. This has led to the myth of the talkative woman—a false idea that still exists today in many cultures despite the fact that the position of women has greatly improved in the last century. When any person, male or female, has social, political, or economic power, their speech is **valued**, not seen as **excessive**. For example, imagine a female prime minister or president. Would anyone complain that she talks too much? Of course not. Most people would respect her words and listen to her carefully. This shows clearly how language and power are closely related to each other.

Turn-of-the-Century Ideas

5 In the late twentieth century, two American scholars[5], Robin Lakoff and Deborah Tannen, researched and wrote about important ideas on language and gender. Robin Lakoff described female speech in her book *Language and Woman's Place*. According to Lakoff, females are less assertive in their speech, avoiding jokes and **profanity**. Lakoff wrote her book in the 1970s, a time when scholars were very interested in the changing position of women in society. They were exploring the idea of sexism, the unfair treatment of women based on a view of them as **inferior**.

6 During the next two decades, Deborah Tannen wrote many popular books, such as *You Just Don't Understand*, that made the public aware of important differences between male and female communication. Like Lakoff, Tannen agreed that women usually speak more politely and less directly than men. For instance, instead of telling someone directly to open a door, a woman will often use a polite question, such as, "Could you please open the door?".

---

[1] **weapon:** an object used to hurt others, such as a gun or knife
[2] **rust:** to turn a reddish-brown color, sometimes because of not being used
[3] **hen:** a female chicken
[4] **rooster:** a male chicken
[5] **scholar:** a person who studies a subject at a very advanced level

Continued on next page

7 Tannen identified female speech as rapport talk, which can be described as using language to build a strong relationship with other females. According to Tannen, females do this by agreeing with each other and discussing their weaknesses and fears. For example, one woman might complain about her problems finding a good job. Her friends will probably agree with her that it is difficult to do this. Then they might talk freely about their own difficulties in this area.

8 In contrast, Tannen described male speech as report talk. This means using language to show their knowledge about common topics such as sports and politics while avoiding discussion of personal problems. For instance, a group of American men at work are more likely to discuss a recent basketball game instead of personal problems. Talking about basketball gives them a chance to show their knowledge as they discuss what they know about different players and scores.

9 A well-known example used by Tannen to show differences in communication styles is that of a husband and wife who are lost and need directions. The wife will usually want to ask someone for directions, which involves admitting weakness and depending on someone's help. The husband, on the other hand, will usually prefer to use a map or GPS and solve the problem by himself. Both Lakoff and Tannen did important work to help us understand how men and women use language differently in the English-speaking world.

10 Another linguist who has looked at female use of language is Jennifer Coates. Some of her work shows how women used language in the past, when people in many societies believed that women were inferior to men. In her book *Women, Men, and Language*, Coates divided women's speech into several categories, which included house talk and scandal talk. House talk is speech that shares information related to taking care of the home, which has been the traditional role of women for many centuries. Scandal talk is speech that includes criticizing other people's behavior and discussing whether it is right or wrong.

11 This idea of scandal talk is similar to Tannen's description of female gossip, the discussion of other people's secrets. Sharing gossip allows a girl or woman to prove that she is close enough to others to know private details about them. Being close to the right people can result in having more power, and this has been especially important for women in situations where power could not be gained in other ways. Coates' work helped us to see how women's language can be influenced by their position in a culture that is controlled by men.

Progress Toward Equality and the Future

12 Deborah Cameron is a linguist who has examined the differences in male and female language and questioned where these differences come from. In contrast to the idea that speech differences are a natural part of gender, Cameron believes that they are based on the fact that men have more power than women in society. In her book *What Language Barrier?*, she disagrees with the idea that women talk more than men and has found that men often **dominate** conversations. Cameron's work is supported by psychologist Janet Hyde, who has studied male and female communication and believes there are more similarities than differences. The **myth** of the talkative woman, it seems, is decreasing in the twenty-first century as more women gain high positions as CEOs, military generals, and even presidents. For Cameron, the idea that women talk more than men do is a negative opinion suggesting that women talk too much. As we have seen before, this idea is based on the **sexist** thinking that women are less important than men.

13 While considering the place of women in the world today, we see that it has greatly improved in many countries in the last century. As women have greater opportunities to gain more power, we may see changes in how they communicate. In the future, there may be fewer differences in how men and women talk than we originally thought. With more progress being made toward gender equality, could the differences between how men and women speak disappear entirely? As we look at ideas on language and gender, we see that speech is more than communication. Who speaks, who listens, and even which language is used to communicate—all of these important questions are related to the expression of power in cultures around the world.

MAIN IDEAS

Write *T* (true) or *F* (false) for each statement. Rewrite the false statements to make them true. Use your notes to help you.

_F_ 1. Ideas on male and female communication have ~~basically stayed the same~~ *changed* throughout time.

____ 2. Women will speak more assertively as they gain more power.

____ 3. Proverbs from several cultures focus on how talkative men are.

____ 4. According to Lakoff and Tannen, men use language more assertively than women.

____ 5. Tannen believes that female speech is focused on showing knowledge.

____ 6. Coates has divided male speech into several categories.

____ 7. In Cameron's opinion, differences in language are based on differences in power.

____ 8. Cameron believes that females are more talkative than males.

DETAILS

1 Choose the best answer for each question. Write the number of the paragraph where you found the answer on the blank line next to each question. Use your notes to help you.

1. What does the essay writer believe about "excessive" speech? ____

   a. It's related to having less power.

   b. It's related to having more power.

   c. It's related to having excessive power.

2. What does a sexist attitude toward women mean? ____

   a. avoiding profanity

   b. treating women unfairly

   c. using language assertively

3. What does "rapport talk" include doing? ____

   a. talking about weakness

   b. discussing the news

   c. telling funny jokes

4. What is discussed in "report talk"? ____

   a. complaints about people's behavior

   b. secrets and fears

   c. impersonal topics such as sports

5. According to Tannen, what is a woman more likely to do? ____

   a. give opinions assertively

   b. ask for directions

   c. talk about the news

6. How does Coates describe a woman complaining about someone's wrong behavior? _____

   a. rapport talk

   b. scandal talk

   c. report talk

7. According to Tannen, why is gossip valuable to girls and women? _____

   a. It is proof of having a close relationship with someone.

   b. It is a way to share secrets about someone.

   c. It shows that one is more powerful than others.

8. How does Cameron believe men and women behave in conversation? _____

   a. Men and women both dominate conversations.

   b. Men are less talkative that women.

   c. Men actually talk more than women.

2 Look at your notes and at your answers in Preview. How did they help you understand the essay?

MAKE INFERENCES 🔍

Inferring Meanings of Proverbs

An **inference** is an **educated guess** about something that is **not directly stated** in a text. Writers sometimes use **proverbs** as a creative **way of suggesting an idea** without directly stating it. To understand a proverb, readers need to **go beyond the exact meaning of words** and think about other possible meanings.

Look at the example and read the explanation.

   "A woman's tongue is her weapon, and she does not let it rust."

What does this proverb mean? Choose the best answer.

a. Women hurt people with their words.

b. Women have very dangerous tongues.

c. Women argue constantly until they win.

*(The best answer is **c**.)*

We know that *tongue* can mean words or language because people use their tongues to speak. A *weapon* is used for fighting. Fighting with words is arguing. People who argue have a chance to get what they want. If a weapon is used constantly, it will not *rust* or get damaged and become useless. **Meaning of proverb:** To get what they want, women talk and argue a lot.

After thinking carefully about the possible meaning of important words in the proverb, we have a better idea of what the whole proverb means. We **can infer** the **meaning of the proverb**.

Remember, proverbs share traditional views that may not reflect the opinion of the modern day. As you discuss the proverbs from the unit, think about how these views have changed over time.

1 Read each proverb. Think carefully about what the important words in the proverb mean. Choose the best meaning of each proverb.

1. "It's an unhappy house where the hen is louder than the rooster."

   a. Men, not women, should control the family.

   b. Families are happy when women talk more than men.

   c. A happy family has a father who talks a lot.

2. "A woman's hair is long, but her tongue is even longer."

   a. Women with long hair talk a lot.

   b. Excessive talking is part of being a woman.

   c. Beautiful women speak too much.

2 Now discuss your answers with a partner. Point out the words, phrases, or statements that helped you find the answers.

DISCUSS 🔍

Work in small groups. Choose one of the questions. Discuss your ideas. Then choose one person in your group to report the ideas to the class.

> **USE YOUR NOTES**
>
> Use your notes to support your answers with information from the reading.

1. What are some ways that power or position affects your communication? (Think of examples from school, home, and work.)

2. Based on the reading, some of the differences in male and female communication may be based on differences in power. What are some other ways that power or position affects our communication? Consider the ways these people communicate with each other: worker / manager, student / teacher, child / parent.

3. What do the three proverbs mentioned in the text have in common? Are there proverbs from your home culture that express a similar view?

🔘 Go to **My**English**Lab** to give your opinion about another question.

READING TWO | The Question of Global English

PREVIEW

1 Look at the title and photos on the next page. Read the first paragraph. Write two questions that you think will be answered in this reading.

_____

_____

2 Look at the boldfaced words in the reading. Which words do you know the meaning of?

1 Read the *Traveling Man* blog, written by a traveler who is interested in different languages and cultures. As you read, guess the meanings of the words that are new to you. Remember to take notes on main ideas and details.

The Question of Global English

Traveling Man—Jason C.—July 17

Hello, fellow travelers.

1   I'm on my way to France through the Spanish Basque country. Last night I saw a big sign at a café reading: *English spoken here*. It got me thinking: Is English as a global language helping people around the world to communicate better? Or is it causing us to lose everything that makes us **unique**? Is it fair to have one powerful language that people around the world have to learn?

2   **Olivia L:** As an American, I like it. People who know English can communicate almost anywhere in the world. As a native speaker of English, I don't have to learn any other languages. At the same time, I sometimes feel embarrassed when I compare myself to people who know English, plus two or three other languages. I feel so stupid sometimes.

3   **Maria F:** Using English as a global language makes sense to me. It's convenient for us to have a common language. We tried Esperanto before, but that didn't spread like English. Language can't be created or forced. It's a natural expression of a culture. As an invented language, Esperanto doesn't have any native culture.

4   **Jason C:** What's Esperanto? Isn't that some kind of spy language from World War II?

5   **Maria F:** Earlier than that—it goes back to the 1880s. A scholar invented it to give people a common language they could all learn easily. He felt that having different languages divides people into enemy groups. He hoped that Esperanto would change things.

6   **Yi-Wen C:** But the grammar of Esperanto is based on European languages, so it's not that easy for non-Europeans to learn. Besides, it's not as cool as speaking English. English is more than a language. It's an attitude, a lifestyle. It's Hollywood, rock and roll.

7   **Vasily Z:** It's all political. Whoever wins a war gets to control the language of the world. But I do agree that it's easier for people to have a common language. So why not English? It's a simple language. If it weren't that easy, how could a billion people around the world have learned it?

Continued on next page

8   **Yuko H:** I don't think it's easy at all. It's taken me years to learn it.

9   **Paola B:** I agree. I hate how the spelling's so complicated, so full of exceptions.

10   **Ashok P:** I like that it has so many **dialects**. You don't have to speak like any one nationality—you have choices.

11   **Ali M:** For me, it was easy to learn English at school in Qatar since I went to an English-speaking school. Now my English is almost perfect. And I started young, so it wasn't too hard to learn.

12   **Yuko H:** I wish I had perfect English. I'm not even close. There's so much **slang**, and so many **synonyms**—it gives me a headache. And why are there so many verb tenses? Do we really need to know the past perfect? Give me Esperanto.

13   **Gorka A**: Try learning Basque if you want a real challenge. English is so much easier!

14   **Jason C:** I'm not so sure now. Thanks for sharing your ideas. I'll post again as soon as I get to France.

2 Compare your notes on main ideas and details with a partner's. How can you improve your notes next time?

Go to the **Pearson Practice English App** or **MyEnglishLab** for more vocabulary practice.

NOTE-TAKING SKILL

Taking Notes with a T-chart

When taking notes, it is often helpful to use a graphic organizer. One simple type of graphic organizer is a T-chart. It looks like the letter T and allows you to compare two different ideas, things, or people. You can also use a T-chart to note pros (+) and cons (–). This will help you to organize information and review for tests and other assignments.

English as a global language	Esperanto as a global language
+ *Americans don't have to learn other langs*	+ *Common lang all people learn easily*
–	–

1 Look at Reading Two and add more pros (+) and cons (–) for using English as a global language.

2 Look at Reading Two again and add more pros (+) and cons (–) for using Esperanto as a global language.

Go to **MyEnglishLab** for more note-taking practice.

COMPREHENSION

1 **Read the statements and mark them *T* (true) or *F* (false). Rewrite the false statements to make them true. Use your notes from Reading Two to help you. Discuss your answers with a partner.**

_____ 1. Most Americans speak several languages.

_____ 2. Esperanto was invented as a language to help people find peace.

_____ 3. There are one billion non-native speakers of English in the world.

_____ 4. English can be difficult because of spelling, vocabulary, and grammar.

_____ 5. Everyone agrees that English is a difficult language to learn.

2 **Review the boldfaced words from the reading with a partner. Use a dictionary or ask your teacher for any meanings you still do not know.**

READING SKILL

1 **In Reading Two, people express their opinions about English as a global language. A strong reader understands how examples and reasons are used to support opinions. Look at paragraph 2. What is Olivia L's opinion of global English? What reasons does she give to support her opinion?**

Recognizing How Examples Support Opinions

Writers sometimes present a variety of opinions in a text. Readers need to understand how **different examples support different opinions.**

Look at these opinions and examples from Reading One:

Opinion 1: Tannen agreed that women usually speak more politely and less directly than men.

Example 1: For instance, instead of telling someone directly to open a door, a woman will often use a polite question, such as, "Could you please open the door?"

Opinion 2: Tannen believes that rapport talk means using language to build a strong relationship with other females by agreeing with each other and discussing weaknesses and fears.

Example 2: For example, one woman might complain about her problems finding a good job. Her friends will probably agree with her that it is difficult to do this.

Again, it is important to read examples carefully and think about their meanings. Remember that the **purpose of an example is to support a main idea.**

2 Work with a partner. Read each opinion from Reading Two. Then match the opinion with a supporting example.

Opinions

_____ 1. As an American, I like global English.

_____ 2. The inventor of Esperanto believed in having a common language.

_____ 3. Language is political.

_____ 4. A grammar based on European languages is difficult for non-Europeans to learn.

_____ 5. A language is easy if a billion people can learn it.

_____ 6. Some languages are more difficult than others.

Supporting Examples

a. Basque

b. English

c. Speakers of English don't have to learn other languages.

d. People who are divided by different languages often fight wars.

e. The world's global language depends on the result of war.

f. Esperanto

Go to **MyEnglishLab** for more skill practice.

CONNECT THE READINGS

ORGANIZE

Reading One (R1) and Reading Two (R2) contain information about the relationship between language and power. Look at the first parts of some statements and write each one under the correct heading in the chart on the next page. Then complete each statement with information from R1 or R2.

> **USE YOUR NOTES**
>
> Review your notes from Reading One and Two. Use the information in your notes to complete the chart.

a. Some view women's speech as excessive because . . .

b. Native speakers of English don't have to . . .

c. One reason English has become a global language is because of . . .

d. As women gain more power in society, their communication might . . .

e. One reason why some women speak more politely than men is that . . .

f. Native and non-native speakers of English can communicate . . .

g. In many cultures, male speech has been more valued than female speech because of . . .

LANGUAGE AND GENDER (R1)	ENGLISH AS A GLOBAL LANGUAGE (R2)
1. *a. Some view women's speech as excessive because . . . it has not been seen as important.*	**1.**
2.	**2.**
3.	**3.**
4.	**4.**

SYNTHESIZE

Complete the paragraph outline with information from Organize. Then use the outline to write a complete paragraph. Remember that the main idea expressed in the topic sentence has a supporting point. Each supporting point has details.

  I. Topic Sentence: The use of language is an expression of power in individual societies and also between nations.

 II. Supporting Point: In most societies, men have had more power than women.

Supporting Details:

A. Male speech = _____ than female speech

B. Female speech = _____ than male speech

C. The myth of the "talkative woman" has been part of many societies _____

_____ .

III. Supporting Point: As a global language, English offers advantages as a tool of communication between nations.

Supporting Details:

A. English has become a global language because of _____ .

B. Native speakers don't have to _____ .

C. Non-native speakers can _____ .

IV. Concluding Sentence: Language use is an expression of power both internationally and also within individual societies.

Go to **MyEnglishLab** to check what you learned.

VOCABULARY

REVIEW

Read the email from a non-native speaker of English to a friend, describing a visit to his American wife's family. Complete the email with words from the box. Use each word only once.

assertive	exception	myth	sexist	synonyms
dialect	excessive	profanity	slang	unique
dominate	inferior	proverb	talkative	valued

Subject:

From: Taka   To: Pedro

Hi Pedro,

I finally have a few free minutes here in Seattle, where we're visiting Ashley's parents. Her two

sisters, Brooke and Lauren, are visiting them, too, so I met the whole family. It's amazing how her

family is so different from mine. First of all, her older sister, Brooke, lives in London and has picked

up the local _____. It's been hard to communicate with her because her
                    1.

pronunciation is tough to understand. She is very funny, but she speaks quickly and uses a lot of

_____ when she tells stories. I thought I knew a lot of English vocabulary, but
         2.

knowing definitions and _____ didn't help because some of the words she uses
                              3.

have totally different meanings. (I thought a "boot" was a type of shoe, but to Brooke, it's part of a

car!) Another thing is that Brooke has a very strong personality. No matter what we're talking about,

she tries to _____ the conversation. I mentioned this to Ashley, and she got mad
                 4.

at me for being so _____. She thinks that men who complain about
                        5.

_____ women are hanging on to the old idea that women are _____
         6.   **7.**

to men. Another difference is that her mom is a lot more _____ than mine. She
                                                                    8.

has her own business and is used to getting things done. After talking to her for a while, I think it's

definitely a _____ that women aren't strong enough to be successful in business.
                 9.

She's a very strong lady—and I think that's part of what makes the family _____.
                                                                                        10.

I've never met a mother like this one before. Also, I'm a bit shocked by Ashley's younger brother, Sam.

Continued on next page

I'm not used to hearing so much _____ from someone his age, especially in front
                                          11.
of his parents. Maybe this is just the way most young people talk, and he is no _____.
                                                                                      12.
Or maybe I was raised with _____ politeness because my parents are a little
                                    13.
old-fashioned. I don't know. Spending time with Ashley's family reminds me of the old

_____ that you don't just marry a person—you marry a person's family, too.
          14.
Anyway, I've had a pretty good time with them. They seem to like me and make me feel like a

_____ part of the family.
          15.
I'll see you in a couple of days when we get back. You can see all my pictures on Instagram.

Taka

EXPAND

1 **Complete the chart with the correct word forms. Use a dictionary if necessary. An X**
  indicates that you do not need to put a word in that category.

	NOUN	VERB	ADJECTIVE	ADVERB
1.	assertiveness		assertive	
2.		dominate		dominantly
3.	exception	×		
4.		×	excessive	
5.		×	inferior	X
6.	myth	×		mythically
7.	profanity	×		X
8.	proverb	×		X
9.		×	sexist	X
10.	synonym	×		X
11.			talkative	
12.	uniqueness	×		
13.			valued	X

2 Match the words on the left with their antonyms (opposites) on the right. Use a dictionary if necessary.

_____ 1. assertiveness

_____ 2. domination

_____ 3. excess

_____ 4. inferiority

_____ 5. mythical

_____ 6. profane

_____ 7. talkativeness

_____ 8. unique

_____ 9. value

a. lack

b. disregard

c. submission

d. silence

e. common

f. real

g. timidity

h. superiority

i. polite

CREATE

APPLY Write a paragraph describing how your friends or family use language. Use six new words from this unit.

Go to the **Pearson Practice English App** or **MyEnglishLab** for more vocabulary practice.

GRAMMAR FOR WRITING

1 Read the conversation between two male friends. How are the boldfaced phrases similar in meaning? How are they different?

ANTONIO: Where's your wife today?

MINH: She's in her English class.

ANTONIO: Doesn't she know a lot of English?

MINH: She does, but she always wants to learn more. I get bored with English. I can't study languages **as hard as** she can.

ANTONIO: My wife is the opposite. She hates learning English.

MINH: Not as much as I do. No one learns English **as slowly as** I do!

ANTONIO: That's not true. You've learned it **more quickly than** anyone I know.

Comparative Adverbs

Comparative adverbs are used to compare the actions expressed by verbs. Adverbs usually end in *-ly,* but there are exceptions such as *hard* and *well.*	Some people study languages more **carefully** than others. *(different)*
	Your mother explains grammar less **patiently** than mine. *(different)*
Actions can be compared by using *as . . . as, not as . . . as, more . . . than,* and *less . . . than*.	My mother learns English **as quickly as** my father. *(equal)*
	My sister **doesn't** learn English **as quickly as** my brother. *(not equal)*
	My brother **doesn't** study English **as hard as** I do. *(not equal)*

2 Complete the paragraph with the comparative form of the adverbs in parentheses.

My sister went to Mexico to learn Spanish. At first, she couldn't speak _____
                                                                                    1. (fluently)

native speakers. Native speakers spoke much _____ she did, so it was difficult
                                                        2. (rapidly)

for her to understand them. She spoke a lot _____ they did, and sometimes she
                                                    3. (slowly)

had to repeat herself. Her goal was to speak Spanish _____ native speakers, so
                                                                4. (well)

she decided to go to language school. There she studied Spanish _____ any other
                                                                        5. (carefully)

student, so her teacher was very proud of her. After two years of studying Spanish and living

in Mexico, she spoke just a little _____ a native speaker. She might never speak
                                            6. (perfectly)

exactly like a native speaker, but she sure sounds good to me!

3 APPLY **Think about the last time you spoke English or another foreign language. How did you speak? How did others react to your speaking? Write four sentences about how you spoke. Use a comparative adverb in each.**

1. _I spoke more slowly than my roommate._

2. _____

3. _____

4. _____

5. _____

Go to the **Pearson Practice English App** or **MyEnglishLab** for more grammar practice. Check what you learned in **MyEnglishLab**.

FINAL WRITING TASK: A Contrast Paragraph 🔍 APPLY

In this unit, you read about the way men and women use language to communicate and how this relates to power.

Now you are going to *write a contrast paragraph focusing on two or three important differences between two kinds of speakers in your home culture. Think of speakers who differ in power: student / teacher, boss / employee, older person / younger person, male / female, and so on.* Be sure to use examples to support each difference.

For an alternative writing topic, see page 97.

PREPARE TO WRITE: Creating a Chart

Use the chart to list some ways that different kinds of speakers use language differently in your home culture. You may consider such differences as topics, gossip, requests, and jokes. See the example below. You may change "males" and "females" to other kinds of speakers (native / non-native, worker / manager, student / teacher, and so on).

	DIFFERENCE 1	DIFFERENCE 2	DIFFERENCE 3	DIFFERENCE 4	DIFFERENCE 5
Males	Use more impolite words				
Females	Avoid using impolite words				

WRITE

Writing a Contrast Paragraph

When **contrasting**, you explain how two or more ideas are **different**. One way to contrast is by using point-by-point organization. When you use point-by-point organization, the points (ideas) in a paragraph are discussed one-by-one.

1 **Read the paragraph and look at the point-by-point outline on the next page. Complete the outline with details and examples from the paragraph.**

When I speak English, the way I speak is different depending on the situation. One important difference is the formality of language. When I'm with my friends at school, I can use more informal language. On the other hand, while shopping, I don't want to be impolite by speaking too informally. For example, when I'm talking to a clerk in the supermarket, I say, "Would you mind putting that in a bag?" This is more polite than saying, "Put that in a bag." Another difference is asking for help. If I know a person well, I feel comfortable asking what a word means or whether I am saying something correctly. However, if I am speaking to a stranger, I don't like asking for help with my English. Sometimes I pretend to understand something that I don't really understand at all. Finally, I try not to use profanity at all, but once in a while, I do with my friends. It is not polite enough for talking with older people or teachers in class. The same is true of slang. It's fun to use with my friends, but older people don't always understand me, so I have to find another way to say what I mean. These are some of the differences in the ways that I use English, my second language.

Point 1: Formality of language

    Details / Examples:

_____

    A. At school:

_____

    B. In the supermarket:

_____

Point 2: Asking for help

    Details / Examples:

_____

    A. Speaking to people the writer knows well:

_____

_____

    B. Speaking to strangers:

_____

_____

Point 3: Profanity / Slang

    Details / Examples:

_____

    A. Talking with friends:

_____

_____

    B. Talking with teachers / older people:

_____

_____

2 **Look at your notes from Prepare to Write on page 93. Write the first draft of your paragraph.**

- Make sure you have a strong topic sentence

- Include two or three supporting points. Each one should focus on a difference. Use comparative adverbs to describe differences. Include details to explain each supporting point.

- Write a concluding sentence that summarizes the differences.

- Use comparative adverbs to compare actions expressed by verbs.

REVISE: Using Transitions of Contrast

1 Read a paragraph about the differences in use of language between two different groups of people. Look at the boldfaced words. What do they mean? Discuss with a partner.

Millennials are the generation of people born from 1981 to 1996. Sometimes, we see difficulties in communication between millennials and people from older generations in the workplace. According to a study, millennials might be seen as communicating less professionally than their older co-workers. **Unlike** office workers from older generations, millennials might prefer to communicate online—using short, informal sentences. Another communication difference is in using formal language to show respect. For most people from older generations, more formal language is used when speaking with bosses and managers. Millennials, **on the other hand**, usually speak to most people at their workplace using similar language. These differences sometimes make it difficult for people from different generations to communicate. **However**, with a little bit of effort, they can learn to understand their differences and have better working relationships.

Transitions of Contrast

Writers use **transitions** to help readers move from one idea to another. Transitions help readers understand the relationship between ideas. A variety of transitions are used to show **contrast** (differences) between ideas.

Some transitions of contrast appear at the beginning of a sentence followed by a comma. They can also be placed between the subject and the verb of a sentence.

Examples of this type of transition include *however* and *on the other hand*.

- Despite these different ways of thinking, **however,** we can see a connection between women's power and how their communication is seen by others.

- I usually think of friends as people I do things with, such as camping or playing sports. My brother, **on the other hand,** usually identifies his friends as people with whom he talks frequently.

Other transitions begin a sentence and are followed by a noun or noun phrase and a comma.

Examples of this type of transition include *unlike* and *in contrast to*.

- **Unlike** millennials, many professionals from older generations use formal language when talking to a boss or manager.

- **In contrast to** older generations, many millennials prefer to communicate using the internet.

2 Look at the paragraph on page 93. Underline the transitions of contrast.

3 Rewrite the sentences. Use the transition words in parentheses. You may need to change or omit some parts of the sentences.

1. My younger sister enjoys playing soccer with her friends. My older sister would rather spend time talking with hers. (*on the other hand*)

   My younger sister enjoys playing soccer with her friends. My older sister, on the other hand,

   would rather spend time talking to hers.

2. The English language ~~has developed as part of a culture~~. Esperanto was developed without any specific culture. (*unlike*)

   unlike _____

3. "Report talk" is a style of communication that is focused on sharing knowledge. "Rapport talk" is focused on building relationships. (*however*)

   _____

4. When I'm at work, I avoid telling jokes and using humor. When I am with my friends, I often tell jokes. (*on the other hand*)

   _____

5. My English class is very informal. The office ~~where I work is very formal~~. (*in contrast to*)

   " " " " " " " " *, in contrast to the office I work in.*

6. Speaking English to people I know well ~~is easy~~. Speaking English to strangers is sometimes difficult. (*in contrast to*)

   In contrast to speaking English to people I know well
   is easy, speaking English to strangers is someti—

4 Now go back to the first draft of your paragraph.

- Add transitions to show the contrast between ideas where possible. Make sure you use the correct transitions and punctuation.

- Try to use the grammar and some of the vocabulary from the unit.

🔵 Go to **My**EnglishLab for more skill practice.

EDIT: Writing the Final Draft

APPLY Write the final draft of your paragraph and submit it to your teacher. Carefully edit it for grammatical and mechanical errors, such as spelling, capitalization, and punctuation. Consider how to apply the vocabulary, grammar, pronunciation, and writing skills from the unit. Use the checklist to help you.

FINAL DRAFT CHECKLIST

☐ Does your paragraph contain a clear topic sentence stating the main idea?

☐ Does it contain two or three important differences?

☐ Are the differences supported by examples and / or details?

☐ Are transitions of contrast used correctly?

☐ Are commas used to punctuate transitions?

☐ Does your paragraph end with a clear concluding sentence?

☐ Does your paragraph include comparative adverbs?

☐ Do you use new vocabulary from the unit?

ALTERNATIVE WRITING TOPIC

APPLY Which languages are spoken in your home culture? Is it important to know English in addition to other languages? Which language is connected with social and economic power? Write a paragraph describing the various languages that are important to people in your home culture. Use the grammar and vocabulary from the unit.

CHECK WHAT YOU'VE LEARNED

Check (✔) the outcomes you've met and vocabulary you've learned. Put an X next to the skills and vocabulary you still need to practice.

Learning Outcomes

☐ **Infer meanings of proverbs**

☐ **Take notes with a T-chart**

☐ **Recognize how examples support opinions**

☐ **Use comparative adverbs**

☐ **Use transitions of contrast**

☐ **Write a contrast paragraph**

Vocabulary

☐ **assertive**

☐ **dialect**

☐ **dominate** AWL

☐ **excessive**

☐ **inferior**

☐ **myth**

☐ **profanity**

☐ **proverb**

☐ **sexist**

☐ **slang**

☐ **synonym**

☐ **talkative**

☐ **unique** AWL

☐ **valued** (*adj.*)

Go to **My**English**Lab** to watch a video about language, access the Unit Project, and take the Unit 4 Achievement Test.

LEARNING OUTCOMES

> Infer when humor is used
> Take notes with bullets
> Predict content from titles and subheadings

> Use future time clauses
> Follow cover letter format
> Write a cover letter

 Go to **MyEnglishLab** to check what you know.

Careers of the Future

1 FOCUS ON THE TOPIC

1. What is a career? What is a job? How are they different?

2. How might careers be different in the future? How will some "old" jobs be replaced by new, different jobs?

3. What are some jobs that will always be important and never disappear?

VOCABULARY

1 Read the advice column from a business newspaper. Pay attention to the boldfaced words.

Ask Danny:
Advice for people wanting to work

Q DEAR DANNY: My job as a film developer is becoming **obsolete** now that everyone takes digital photos. I would like to work for myself as a photographer, but I don't know where to start. Can you advise me on steps I need to take to become a successful **freelancer**? —FUTURE FREELANCER

A DEAR FUTURE FREELANCER: First of all, becoming a freelancer does not mean that you can stay in your pajamas all day and work when you want. As a freelancer, you have to do everything—get the work, do the work, and collect pay for the work. It's very hard! But here are some basic **strategies** to follow if you are determined to try:

1. Create a website with a blog and be sure to add at least one new photo and some comments about it every day. It's very important to have a social media presence.

2. Decide what types of companies have the photography jobs you want and contact the most likely person to hire photographers at those companies. Don't be afraid to make the first contact. People can't hire you if they don't know about you.

3. Respond to emails, phone calls, and social media questions quickly.

4. Take every job that is offered—even the ones that bore you or scare you.

In order to keep a freelance career **sustainable**, you have to work hard for a very long time. And it doesn't offer the job **security** you'd have being on staff at a company, but you will be doing something you love.

DEAR DANNY: I found out today that my job will be **outsourced** next year. The **prospects** for getting another job at my age are few. My hobby is growing flowers, and I'd like to start my own shop with the money I've saved over the years.—FUTURE FLORIST

DEAR FUTURE FLORIST: Using your own money to start a shop is very uncertain. Even the most experienced **entrepreneurs** do not put all their money into one business. So, my first piece of advice is to find some partners to share the risk.

Then ask yourself these questions:

1. Are you certain you could be an **expert** in growing and arranging flowers professionally?

2. Do you have a location in mind?

3. Have you found a supplier[1]?

4. Do you have the necessary licenses and insurance policies?

5. Do you have a marketing plan for your new shop?

6. Are you prepared to work long hours, seven days a week, and on holidays?

When you can answer "yes" to these questions, you can begin.

---

[1] **supplier:** a company or person that provides a particular product

2 Choose the correct synonym for each boldfaced word.

1. Post office workers are worried that their jobs may become **obsolete**. It's so easy to connect with others online that people don't need to send letters or pay bills through the mail anymore.

   a. recent   b. unnecessary

2. **Freelancers** work for themselves, doing projects for different companies.

   a. independent workers   b. retired workers

3. College graduates need a **strategy** for finding a career. They need to prepare for their working lives.

   a. résumé   b. plan

4. Most people can work 15-hour days for a week or two, but working longer is not **sustainable** if product quality is to remain high.

   a. likely to continue   b. tiring

5. In Japan, the **security** of having the same job for your whole life used to be very common. Workers never worried about losing their jobs.

   a. protection from change   b. wanting change

6. Companies **outsource** the production of goods as well as service jobs. For example, my brother lost his job making tires when his company moved jobs to Bangladesh.

   a. move workers to another place   b. move jobs to another place

7. The **prospects** for careers in the health field are excellent because there are many more aging people who will need care.

   a. possibilities   b. predictions

8. To be a successful **entrepreneur**, you must be willing to take a risk with your money and your future. You must be independent and believe in your ability to grow a profitable company.

   a. person with a new business idea   b. person with a job

9. Computer programming **experts** will always be needed because their talent and knowledge are important for all types of businesses.

   a. knowledgeable people   b. unaware people

Go to the **Pearson Practice English App** or **MyEnglishLab** for more vocabulary practice.

PREVIEW

You are going to read a blog about the best careers for today's fast-changing workplace. Before you read, look at the list of possible topics. Check (✓) the four topics that you think you will read about.

☐ 1. How to find the perfect employer   ☐ 4. How to adapt to the new job market

☐ 2. What kind of job to look for after college   ☐ 5. What to do when you lose your job

☐ 3. How to become an entrepreneur   ☐ 6. How to find a job with security

READ

Read the blog about today's careers on the next page. Create a chart like the one below to take notes. On the left, put the main ideas. On the right, put the details.

TAKE NOTES

Main Ideas	Details
1 job 4 life—not sustainable (likely to continue)	1 reason = tech: skills will be obsolete / unnecessary

Go to **MyEnglishLab** to view example notes.

Meet Your New Boss: YOU

1. People used to be born into a family business or a family career. You'd follow your dad into the sea, the farm, or the workshop. You'd follow your mom into the kitchen or sewing room. In your grandparents' time, there was the **prospect** of working a job from graduation until retirement. How times have changed! Most of my friends do not plan to follow in their parents' footsteps[1] or even to stay in one job for very long. Working at one particular job for the rest of your life just isn't **sustainable**.

2. In fact, planning to work in the same field or industry for your entire working life just isn't practical anymore. One reason for this is technology. Skills you learn today will be **obsolete** very soon. And then what will you do? Work hard? Win the lottery? Hope for the best or pray? You might be lucky. These **strategies** might bring you a nice, comfy life, working at a job you like and retiring while you're still young and healthy enough to enjoy it. But most of us working today have to look beyond the little box of "career." This means thinking of new ways to make our own money and constantly learning to stay on top of this technology we love and hate and use for everything.

3. If you think you can work eight hours a day and build a career, think again. If you think you can't be replaced by **artificial intelligence (AI)** or have your job **outsourced** to the moon, you are wrong. An employer can always replace you or find someone who can do your job more cheaply. One way to protect yourself is to take what you do at the office and do it on your own as a **freelancer** for a limited time without a contract. For example, if your job is to edit advertising copy all day, you are developing (and getting good at) a skill that other people want. Editing is a skill that most companies need some of the time. These companies may not offer full-time employment, but they have 100 hours of work that needs to be done now. You step in, get the job done, and make some extra money. You may even find that you make more money as a freelancer and are able to quit your full-time job (before it is outsourced).

4. Another strategy is to find something to do besides what you're doing and keep finding a smarter way to do it. That could be turning a hobby into a small business or using your skills to create products and services that you can sell. In other words, think like an **entrepreneur**. Find someone who is willing to help you make your idea a reality. You'll need money, organization, workers, and a lot of energy. You'll need to be a risk taker, an innovator,[2] a problem solver, and a hard worker. Being an entrepreneur is not an 8-hour-a-day job; it is a 24-hour-a-day job. And when things go well, you have your rewards. Here's an example. A woman I grew up with decided to become a chef. Then she developed a wedding cake business. A few years later, she started blogging about desserts and writing restaurant reviews for a website. One thing can lead to another, especially if you become an **expert** at something.

5. Jobs and careers come and go at an amazing pace these days. What if your job disappears after working for 10 years in the field? You may have to go back to school to be able to work in a completely different field. You may have to retrain yourself in order to keep working at the same company or in the same field. In fact, in all likelihood, you will have to do this more than once.

6. In short, if you are going to succeed in the twenty-first-century job market, you have to broaden your idea of what earning a living is. Lifetime **security** from one employer is no longer certain or even likely. The truth is that you will probably have several jobs in different fields in your lifetime; you may even work as a freelancer or form your own company. Are you ready for this new type of career? It's definitely ready for you!

---

[1] **follow in somebody's footsteps:** to do the same job that someone else did before you
[2] **innovator:** someone who introduces changes and new ideas

MAIN IDEAS

Read the statements. They all give bad career advice. Rewrite each statement to reflect one of the main ideas of the reading. Use your notes to help you.

1. If you find the right job, you can work there for your entire career.

   _____

2. Most employers offer job security to their employees.

   _____

3. If you lose your job and can't find a new one, you can easily become an entrepreneur.

   _____

4. Becoming an expert in one job is enough to support you.

   _____

DETAILS

1 To paraphrase a sentence means to say it in a different way, using your own words. These sentences are paraphrases of sentences in the blog. Write the exact sentence from the blog that has the same meaning as the paraphrase. Look at the paragraph number in parentheses. Use your notes to help you.

1. Years ago, you could start working in one place and work there all your life. *(paragraph 1)*

   In your grandparents' time, there was the prospect of working a job from graduation
   until retirement.

2. The abilities you have today won't be needed in the future. *(paragraph 2)*

   _____

3. Most workers have to think of more than just one type of job. *(paragraph 2)*

   _____

4. Your boss could hire someone to do your job for less money. *(paragraph 3)*

   _____

5. Develop an independent skill and try to do it differently and better than others. *(paragraph 4)*

   _____

6. You'll need a partner who wants you to succeed. *(paragraph 4)*

   _____

7. Taking chances, being creative, thinking of solutions, and being tireless are what you need. *(paragraph 4)*

   _____

2 Look at your notes and at your answers in Preview. How did they help you understand the blog?

MAKE INFERENCES 🔍

Inferring When Humor Is Used

An **inference** is an **educated guess** about something that is **not directly stated** in a text. Writers sometimes use **humor** (sarcasm, exaggeration, and jokes), and the reader must use inference to understand that the writer is not being serious and is making a point indirectly by using humor.

Look at the example and read the explanation.

"And then what will you do? Work hard? Win the lottery? Hope for the best or pray?"

In this text, the author offers suggestions of what to do if your job becomes obsolete, but none of the strategies are realistic:

Work hard? Here the author is being **sarcastic,** saying that you might be a very hard worker, but it's hard to work hard when your job is gone.

Win the lottery? Here the author is **exaggerating** because very few people win the lottery.

Hope for the best or pray? And here, the author is **joking**. Everyone knows that getting a new job requires more than hoping and praying.

After reading the text closely, we can **infer** that the author is using **humor**.

1 **Check (✓) the phrases and sentences from the reading that show humor. Then discuss your answers with a partner. Look at the paragraphs in parentheses. Explain the examples of humor.**

☐ 1. Skills you learn today will be obsolete very soon. (*paragraph 2*)

☐ 2. You might be lucky. These strategies might bring you a nice, comfy life. (*paragraph 2*)

☐ 3. Look beyond the little box of "career." (*paragraph 2*)

☐ 4. This means constantly learning to stay on top of this technology. (*paragraph 2*)

☐ 5. If you think you can work eight hours a day and build a career, think again. (*paragraph 3*)

☐ 6. If you think you can't be replaced by artificial intelligence (AI) or have your job outsourced to the moon, you are wrong. (*paragraph 3*)

☐ 7. You are developing (and getting good at) a skill that other people want. (*paragraph 3*)

☐ 8. Quit your job (before it is outsourced). (*paragraph 3*)

☐ 9. Find someone who is willing to help you make your idea a reality. (*paragraph 4*)

☐ 10. Being an entrepreneur is not an 8-hour-a-day job; it is a 24-hour-a-day job. (*paragraph 4*)

2 **Now discuss your answers with a partner. Point out the words, phrases, or statements that helped you find the answers.**

Work in small groups. Choose one of the questions below. Discuss your ideas. Then choose one person in your group to report the ideas to the class.

USE YOUR NOTES

Use your notes to support your answers with information from the reading.

1. What skills and qualities does a person need to become an entrepreneur?

2. Consider your chosen skill. What are some options for freelancing?

3. Which jobs are more likely / less likely to be done by machines in coming years? Why?

🔾 Go to **MyEnglishLab** to give your opinion about another question.

READING TWO | Great Jobs for the Twenty-First Century

PREVIEW

1 Look at the photo below and the title on the next page. Read the first paragraph. Write two questions that you think will be answered in this reading.

_____

_____

2 Look at the boldfaced words in the reading. Which words do you know the meaning of?

READ

1 Read the information from a career center on the next page. As you read, guess the meanings of the words that are new to you. Remember to take notes on main ideas and details.

2 After you finish reading, compare your notes on main ideas and details with a partner's. How can you improve your notes next time?

Great Jobs for the Twenty-first Century

Social Media Managers
At the start of the twenty-first century, there was no Facebook, Twitter, or Instagram. But companies today have to plan strategies for using social media to communicate with customers and to advertise their products. They will always need experts who understand the **benefits** of staying in touch.

Health Care Professionals
As the population ages and treatments for disease become more comprehensive, there will be continuing high demand for doctors and nurses. Compared to other doctors, dentists are retiring in record numbers, and there are not enough new dentists to replace them. And that means there will also be many job opportunities for dental assistants to help with the extra work.

Sustainability Directors
The goal of sustainability is to make sure that natural resources, such as land and water, will be available to future generations. As companies become more concerned about the environment, they will look to sustainability directors to help them reduce waste and pollution by finding more earth-friendly ways of producing, storing, and selling goods.

Experts in Artificial Intelligence
With the huge popularity of online games, this career attracts many and is not limited to entertainment. Improving technology can also be used in training, education, and therapy. Jobs in this field are available to artists as well as to experts in artificial intelligence.

Biomedical Engineers
As the science of biotechnology develops, more biomedical engineers will be needed. People are living longer, partly due to advances in biomedical engineering. A biomedical engineer applies the principles and design of engineering to medicine, primarily in the fields of genetic engineering and brain mapping.

Asteroid Mining Engineers
In the twenty-first century, new technologies will be used to explore space and to look for important resources, including metals and water. Asteroids, the rocky masses located between Mars and Jupiter, have both. As entrepreneurs plan the mining of asteroid resources, mining engineers will be needed to plan, manage, and execute these complex projects.

Cybersecurity Experts
The role of a cybersecurity expert is to **ensure** the safety and privacy of personal information collected by institutions such as universities and banks. Both business and tech majors will enjoy making sure that hackers and thieves are stopped by finding out their methods.

Physical and Occupational Therapists
When people break a bone or are **injured**, their lives are upset in many ways. Physical therapists help to heal the physical injury, and occupational therapists train the patient to live a normal life again. These important jobs will always be necessary.

Astrophysicists
In the twenty-first century, the exploration of space will become more and more common and **critical**. And in order to explore space, an understanding of the universe and its physical properties is necessary. Astrophysicists study the universe's physical properties such as density, temperature, and chemical makeup, and then analyze the data. With more countries—and private companies—investigating the universe, the demand for astrophysicists will continue to rise.

Go to the **Pearson Practice English App** or **My**English**Lab** for more vocabulary practice.

Taking Notes with Bullets

When taking notes, it is often helpful to make lists with bullet points. This helps you to identify key information about a variety of things or ideas. Focusing on this information will help you prepare for tests and other assignments. It may also help you make critical comparisons between two or more things or ideas. Sometimes you can use *wh*-words such as *Who, What, When, Where, Why,* and *How*. In the chart below, use "Why?" for the question "Why are they needed?" and use "What?" for the question "What will they do?"

Social Media Managers

- Why? *Help companies communicate w/ customers*
- What? *Facebook / Twitter / Instagram—advertising.*

Experts in Artificial Intelligence

- Why? *Popularity of games*
- What? *Improve tech. 4 entertainment, training, educ. & therapy*

1 Add information to complete the notes for each job.

Cybersecurity Experts

- Why? *To stop hackers and* _____
- What? *Ensure safety & privacy of* _____

Health Care Professionals

- Why? *Not enough new dentists, high demand 4* _____
- What? *Help w/* _____

Biomedical Engineers

- Why? *Dev. of* _____
- What? *Apply engineering to* _____

  Ex: genetic engineering, _____

2 Create notes for each job.

Physical and Occupational Therapists

- Why? _____
- What? _____

Sustainability Directors

- Why? _____
- What? _____

Asteroid Mining Engineers

- Why? _____
- What? _____

  _____

Astrophysicists

- Why? _____

- What? _____

 Go to **My**English**Lab** for more note-taking practice.

COMPREHENSION

1 Read the statements and mark them _T_ (true) or _F_ (false). Rewrite the false statements to make them true. Use your notes from Reading Two to help you. Discuss your answers with a partner.

_____ 1. Experts in artificial intelligence are not limited to developing entertainment.

_____ 2. Cybersecurity experts only work for businesses.

_____ 3. The field of biomedical engineering started because people are living longer.

_____ 4. Sustainability directors help companies be more earth-friendly.

_____ 5. Astrophysicists are interested in finding water in space.

2 Review the boldfaced words from the reading with a partner. Use a dictionary or ask your teacher for any meanings you still do not know.

READING SKILL

1 Look at Reading Two again. How many subheadings does it have?

Predicting Content from Titles and Subheadings

One way to predict the content of a text is to look at its title and subheadings:

- A good **title** is a brief **summary of the main idea of the whole reading**.

- A good **subheading** is a brief **summary of the content of a section** of the reading.

Look at the title and subheadings of Reading Two and read the explanations.

- The **title** ("Great Jobs for the Twenty-first Century") indicates the main idea of the reading.

- **The subheadings** give you more specific information about that topic: the names of several kinds of jobs. By reading the subheadings, you can find the group of jobs that you are interested in and focus your attention quickly on those.

2 Read the subheadings from Reading Two again quickly. Think about which job category they belong in, and write them in the columns. Compare your answers with a partner's.

COMPUTERS	MEDICINE	SPACE	ENVIRONMENT
social media managers			

🔵 Go to **My**English**Lab** for more skill practice.

CONNECT THE READINGS 🔍

ORGANIZE

Reading One (R1) and Reading Two (R2) contain information about a variety of careers. Look at the chart listing some of the features mentioned in Reading One and some of the jobs mentioned in Reading Two. Check (✓) the box if you believe the job has that feature, and put an X if the job does not.

> **USE YOUR NOTES**
>
> Review your notes from Reading One and Two. Use the information in your notes to complete the chart.

R1 / R2	JOB SECURITY	POSSIBILITY OF BEING OUTSOURCED	OPPORTUNITIES FOR ENTREPRENEURS	OPPORTUNITIES FOR FREELANCERS
Social media managers	X	✓	✓	✓
Experts in artificial intelligence				
Cybersecurity experts				
Health care professionals				
Biomedical engineers				
Asteroid mining engineers				
Astrophysicists				

SYNTHESIZE

Work with a partner to complete an email from a student to his parents explaining why he has changed his career plans. Use information from the chart in Organize.

Subject:

From: 👤 Ali   To: 👤 Mom   ↩ 🗑

Hi Mom,

Everything is great at school. As soon as I got here, I was excited to learn about different careers. I

am writing to tell you that I have changed my plans. I know that you want me to be a doctor because

of the job security. No one can outsource a doctor's job. I also know that in the future, health care

professionals will _____. Unfortunately,
                                              1.
becoming a doctor means spending time and money to get more education, so I looked at

_____. It was interesting to learn about
                          2.
careers related to space like _____. But
                                                        3.
you know that I love games, so now I think that a job as a game developer

_____. This job would also give me a
                          4.
chance to work at home. Maybe _____.
                                                          5.

I would love to know what you think about all of this. Let's talk next week.

Love,

Ali

🔼 Go to **MyEnglishLab** to check what you learned.

REVIEW

Read the essay about jobs and careers in the United States during the last century. Complete the essay with words from the box.

benefits	experts	obsolete	security
ensure	freelancers	outsourced	strategies
entrepreneur	injured	prospects	sustainable

Jobs and Careers in the United States (1900–2000)

Not surprisingly, the job market is changing today as it has done since people started working for other people. The workforce and working conditions especially changed during the twentieth century.

In 1900, most workers farmed or produced goods for sale. Employers weren't looking for

_____ in farming or producing goods. The only job requirements for these jobs were a
1.

healthy body and a willingness to work hard.

At that time, women were only 19 percent of the total number of workers, and children under 15

were 6 percent of workers. The work week was 53 hours, and you probably wouldn't keep your job for

more than a year. So, the _____ for long-term employment were not good. The
2.

working conditions weren't safe, and accidents were very common, causing some workers to be

_____ on the job. In some dangerous industries, such as mining or railroad, workers
3.

were even killed. Wages were comparatively low, and there was no sick pay if you had to miss a day

or more of work. There was no health insurance that would pay your bills if you were hurt on the job.

And if you were out too long, your boss might hire someone else, so the idea of job

_____ didn't really exist. Bosses didn't think there were _____ to
4. 5.

keeping workers because there were always other people eager to work.

In 1900, no one used the word _____, but rich people invested their money in
6.

their own ideas or in other people's. As long as they could _____ a profit[1] they were
7.

---

[1] **profit:** money that you gain by selling things or doing business

willing to pay money to start a business. Women often had to stay at home with their children, but they could earn money by sewing or cooking for others in their homes. They didn't call themselves

_____, but that's what they were.
  8.

In the second half of the century, many jobs such as milkman and iceman became

_____. People didn't need to have milk delivered every day, and they had electric
  9.

refrigerators, so they didn't need ice to keep things cold at home. At the same time, other occupations grew at a quick rate. Later in the century, service industry jobs increased by 47 percent. And because people began to be concerned about developing _____ use of the Earth's resources,
  10.

jobs related to protecting the environment also increased. In the latter part of the century, computers and the internet became commonplace, and skilled technicians were needed to both run and repair them. Across industries, the number of entrepreneurs has increased, and more people are now working as full-time freelancers. In fact, it is estimated that by the year 2030, 60% of the workforce will be freelancers.

As the century closed, jobs were being eliminated or _____ to other countries at
  11.

an increasing rate. It was becoming clear that workers needed to find new ways to earn money and

new _____ for finding jobs. They had to design careers that would support them for
  12.

their whole lives.

EXPAND

1 Complete the chart with the adjective form of the words. Use a dictionary if necessary.

	NOUN / VERB	ADJECTIVE
1.	benefit	beneficial
2.	entrepreneur	
3.	expert	
4.	occupation	
5.	prospect	
6.	strategy	
7.	sustain	

2 Match the adjectives on the left with a noun on the right to make a common expression. The definition of the expression is in parentheses.

_b_ 1. beneficial

_____ 2. entrepreneurial

_____ 3. expert

_____ 4. occupational

_____ 5. prospective

_____ 6. strategic

_____ 7. sustainable

a. employer (someone who might hire you)

b. relationship (good for two people)

c. growth (growth that continues itself)

d. hazard (an injury that happens when you're working)

e. location (the best location to be at a certain time)

f. spirit (full of ideas to make money)

g. advice (suggestions from knowledgeable people in a particular field)

3 Write the expressions you made in Exercise Two. You will need them for the next activity.

1. _____ _beneficial relationship_ _____

2. _____

3. _____

4. _____

5. _____

6. _____

7. _____

CREATE

APPLY **Complete the email to a software company from a recent college graduate who is looking for a job. The graduate is writing to the personnel director, who has advertised for several software design jobs. Use four expressions from Expand, Exercise Three.**

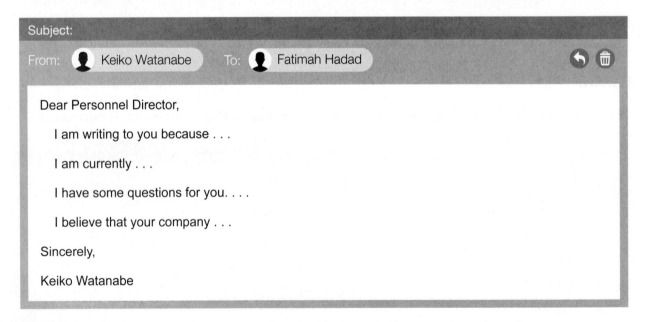

Subject:

From: Keiko Watanabe   To: Fatimah Hadad

Dear Personnel Director,

I am writing to you because . . .

I am currently . . .

I have some questions for you. . . .

I believe that your company . . .

Sincerely,

Keiko Watanabe

Go to the **Pearson Practice English App** or **My**English**Lab** for more vocabulary practice.

GRAMMAR FOR WRITING

1 Read these sentences. Look at the boldfaced verbs. What is the difference between the verb forms? Notice the words that are also italic. What do those words mean?

- *As* more dentists **retire**, there **will not be** enough new dentists to replace them.

- *When* entrepreneurs **plan** the mining of asteroid resources, they **will need** mining engineers to make decisions and provide direction.

- *Before* the company **hires** you, they **will do** a security check of your background.

Future Time Clauses

1. **Future time clauses** show the time relationship between **two future events**:
 	
  • the verb in the **main clause** is in the **future** *(will* or *going to)*
 	
  • the verb in the **time clause** is in the **present**
 	
BE CAREFUL! Do NOT use *will* or *be going to* in the time clause.
 	
The **time clause** starts with a **time expression** like *before* or *when*. The time clause can be at the beginning or at the end of the sentence.
	Main Clause
	They **will check** your background
	Time Clause
	before they **hire** you.
	
	NOT: before they ~~will~~ hire you
	
	Time Clause Main Clause
	When things **go** well, you **will be** rewarded.
	
	NOT: When things ~~will~~ go well

2. When the **time clause** comes at the **beginning** of the sentence, put a **comma** after the time clause. Do NOT use a comma if it comes at the end.	*After* the new company opens**,** many people will apply for jobs. I will apply *when* the jobs are posted. NOT: I will apply*,* when the jobs are posted.

3. These common **time expressions** are used to begin time clauses:
 	
  a. *when, after, as soon as* (to introduce the event that happened first)
 	
  b. *before, by the time* (to introduce the event that happens second)
 	
  c. *while* (to introduce an event that will happen at the same time as another event)
	
	As soon as my report is finished, I'm going to go home.
	
	By the time the sun comes up tomorrow, I will be finished with my report.
	
	While I am writing, I will use spell check.

2 **Complete the conversation with the correct form of the verbs in parentheses. Notice that some sentences are questions.**

TINA: Are you ready for your job interview tomorrow?

SUE: I'm not sure. What happens at a job interview? I've never had one.

TINA: Really? Here's what will probably happen. As soon as you _____ ,
1. (enter)

people _____ at you. Be professional, and dress well. While you are
2. (look)

waiting, you may get nervous. Try to relax. Take a deep breath.

SUE: OK. When I _____ nervous, I _____ a deep breath.
3. (be)   4. (take)

TINA: Right. The first question the interviewers will ask will probably be general. They will ask

you to describe yourself and your experience. Also, interviewers always ask about your

strengths and weaknesses. So, what _____ when the interviewer
5. (you / say)

_____ you about these? Have you thought about this?
6. (ask)

SUE: No! But I _____ about it before I _____ tomorrow.
7. (think)   8. (go)

TINA: The interviewers will ask you why you want the job. They will also want to know what

you know about their company.

SUE: Oh no! When I _____ that answer, what _____ ?
9. (know / not)   10. (the interviewers / do)

TINA: I don't know, but you probably won't make a good impression.

SUE: OK. Before I _____ on the interview, I _____
11. (go)   12. (learn)

about the company. I'm going to start researching right now.

TINA: Good idea.

3 **Combine the two sentences by using the time expression in parentheses. Pay attention to comma use. For items 1–4, put the time clause at the beginning of the sentence. For items 5–8, put the main clause at the beginning of the sentence.**

1. (before)

    • The year will end.

    • Ten percent of the employees will lose their jobs.

    Before the year ends, 10 percent of the employees will lose their jobs.

2. (when)

    • The new boss will arrive.

    • We will be on our best behavior.

    _____

3. (as soon as)

- Ms. Lee will interview prospective employees.
- Ms. Lee will have time.

_____

4. (while)

- We will be in the office.
- We will check the numbers.

_____

5. (after)

- The office party will end.
- Who will clean up?

_____

6. (when)

- We will drive to work.
- We will pick up your friend.

_____

7. (before)

- You will start your own business.
- You will hire someone to help you.

_____

8. (as soon as)

- Our business will make enough money.
- We will open another store.

_____

Go to the **Pearson Practice English App** or **MyEnglishLab** for more grammar practice.
Check what you learned in **MyEnglishLab**.

In this unit, you read about what careers will be like in the future and also learned about some examples of those careers.

Now you are going to *write a cover letter for a prospective employer*. The job you will apply for is your ideal job. Use the vocabulary and grammar from the unit.

For an alternative writing topic, see page 123.

PREPARE TO WRITE: Freewriting

Freewriting is a **technique that writers use to help them gather ideas**. When you use this technique, you write **as much as you can about the topic** you will discuss in your paragraph or essay. You shouldn't worry about word choice, grammar, spelling, or punctuation. No one will see your freewriting except you. Just keep writing, and when you are finished, you can choose ideas and then expand on them.

Freewrite for 10 minutes about your ideal job. Don't evaluate—just write.

WRITE

Structuring a Cover Letter

A cover letter has three parts: an **introduction, supporting points,** and a **conclusion**. The specific content for each part is specific to the job you are applying for, but the basic content is the same for all cover letters.

Introductory paragraph

In this paragraph, introduce yourself and express interest in a specific position in the company. Be clear in your purpose for writing, and be brief.

Supporting paragraph(s)

In this paragraph, you need to focus on your experience and how it will meet the needs of the company. If you can, give specific examples of how you have completed projects and solved problems. Do not write more than two paragraphs. Since employers have to read many cover letters, being brief is important.

Concluding paragraph

This paragraph sums up your interest in the position. Include a reference to the résumé that you have enclosed and your availability for an interview. Be sure to thank the employer for reading your letter with a phrase such as "Thank you for your attention."

1 Read the cover letter and answer the questions.

1. Identify the three parts of a cover letter.

2. Does each part follow the guidelines you read about in Structuring a Cover Letter? Underline examples of places in the letter where the guidelines are followed.

CHRIS YOUNG

47 E. Tempe Road
Tempe, AZ 85281
602-123-4567
chris@xyz.com

January 2, 2019

Thomas L. Jones
Personnel Director
Planetary Resources
350 S. Madison Ave.
Bellevue, WA 98004
tlj@planetaryresources.org

Dear Mr. Jones,

I am writing to apply because the job title "General Space Nut" seems to be the kind of job I would greatly enjoy while I begin my career. And your company is the type of place I'm looking for to get started. I believe I have the qualifications that you're seeking and would be interested in knowing more about your organization.

When I graduate in May with a doctorate in geology and mining from the University of Arizona's Department of Planetary Sciences, I will move to Washington, where I hope to work with you. So, let me tell you a little bit about myself: I was the teenager who was out exploring the desert instead of doing homework, and I was (still am) crazy about rocks. As a graduate student, I led field trips to deserts in Arizona and California to study the rock formations. Adding the study of asteroids to the study of earth geology would be an incredibly exciting challenge for me after I find the appropriate position. I believe that asteroid mining is the way of the future, and I want to devote my career to it.

In short, I am eager to learn more about Planetary Resources and how I can fit into the organization. I am a person who would add to the successes you have and figure out the challenges. When I become a "general space nut," I will do everything I can to advance our understanding of asteroids. I have enclosed a résumé with more details about myself, and I will be happy to meet with you as soon as you review my qualifications. Thank you for your attention.

Sincerely,

Chris Young

Chris Young

2 Look at the freewriting exercise you did in Prepare to Write on page 118. Check (✓) the content areas for each paragraph, and make notes about each from your freewriting. Add information for areas you didn't include in your freewriting or where you don't have enough detail. Use future time clauses where necessary.

Introductory Paragraph:

☐ introduce self _____

☐ identify job _____

☐ state purpose _____

Supporting Paragraph:

☐ discuss experience _____

☐ relate experience to the position / company _____

☐ describe specific example(s) _____

Concluding Paragraph:

☐ summarize your interest _____

☐ refer to enclosed résumé _____

☐ indicate availability for interview _____

☐ thank employer _____

3 Look back at your freewriting in Prepare to Write on page 118. Write the first draft of your letter.

- Make sure your letter has three paragraphs.

- Follow the format in the sample on page 119.

- Use future time clauses to show the relationship between future events.

REVISE: Following Cover Letter Format

1 Look at the cover letter in Prepare to Write. Who is sending the letter? Who is receiving it? How do you know?

Cover Letter Format

In addition to the three parts you studied above, a cover letter format includes **your address, the date, the inside address, the greeting,** and **the closing**.

- **Your address** should be placed on the upper right-hand side of the letter. Include your email address after your phone number.

- Leave one space and put **the date**.

- Leave one space, and put **the inside address** at the left-hand margin. The inside address is the name, position, address, phone number, and email address of the person you are writing to.

- **The greeting** (also called **the salutation**) is the opening to the letter.

  - If you know the name of the person, write

    Dear Mr. Smith,

    Dear Ms. Smith,

  - If you are not sure whether the person is a man or a woman, write the full name.

    Dear Chris Young,

  - If you don't have the name of a specific person, you can write the title of the position.

    Dear Personnel Director,

  - If you don't have any information, you can write a generic greeting.

    To whom it may concern,

- **The closing** is a short phrase followed by your signature.

  Sincerely,

  Respectfully yours,

2 Write the parts of the letter format in the correct place.

| a. closing | b. inside address | c. your address | d. greeting | e. date |

```
_____

_____

_____


        Xxxxxxxxxxxxxxxxxxxxxxxxxxxxxxxxxxxxxxxxxxxxxxx

xxxxxxxxxxxxxxxxxxxxxxxxxxxxxxxxxxxxxxxxxxxxxxxxxxxxxxx

xxxxxxx.
        Xxxxxxxxxxxxxxxxxxxxxxxxxxxxxxxxxxxxxxxxxxxxxxx

xxxxxxxxxxxxxxxxxxxxxxxxxxxxxxxxxxxxxxxxxxxxxxxxxxxxxxx

xxxxxxx.
        Xxxxxxxxxxxxxxxxxxxxxxxxxxxxxxxxxxxxxxxxxxxxxxx

xxxxxxxxxxxxxxxxxxxxxxxxxxxxxxxxxxxxxxxxxxxxxxxxxxxxxxx

xxxxxxx.

_____
```

3 Now go back to the first draft of your cover letter.

- Make sure you used the correct cover letter format.
- Try to use the grammar and some of the vocabulary from the unit.

Go to **MyEnglishLab** for more skill practice.

EDIT: Writing the Final Draft

APPLY Write the final draft of your cover letter and submit it to your teacher. Carefully edit it for grammatical and mechanical errors, such as spelling, capitalization, and punctuation. Consider how to apply the vocabulary, grammar, and writing skills from the unit. Use the checklist to help you.

FINAL DRAFT CHECKLIST

☐ Does your cover letter contain a brief introductory paragraph that clearly explains why you're writing?

☐ Does the introductory paragraph include the name of the position?

☐ Does the supporting paragraph focus on how your skills would meet the employer's needs?

☐ Does the supporting paragraph contain one or two specific examples?

☐ Does the concluding paragraph summarize why you want the job? Does it thank the employer?

☐ Does your letter have correct cover letter format?

☐ Are there future time clauses with verbs in the correct form?

☐ Do these clauses have the correct punctuation?

☐ Do you use new vocabulary from the unit?

ALTERNATIVE WRITING TOPIC

APPLY Write a paragraph describing another career that you think will be common in the future. Give reasons to explain why this type of job will be important and whether or not it can be done by a freelancer or entrepreneur. Use grammar and vocabulary from the unit.

CHECK WHAT YOU'VE LEARNED

Check (✔) the outcomes you've met and vocabulary you've learned. Put an X next to the skills and vocabulary you still need to practice.

Learning Outcomes
☐ **Infer when humor is used**
☐ **Take notes with bullets**
☐ **Predict content from titles and subheadings**
☐ **Use future time clauses**
☐ **Follow cover letter format**
☐ **Write a cover letter**

Vocabulary
☐ **benefit (n.)** AWL
☐ **ensure** AWL
☐ **entrepreneur**
☐ **expert (n.)** AWL
☐ **freelancer**
☐ **injured** AWL

☐ **obsolete**
☐ **outsource**
☐ **prospect (n.)** AWL
☐ **security** AWL
☐ **strategy** AWL
☐ **sustainable** AWL

Go to **MyEnglishLab** to watch a video about careers, access the Unit Project, and take the Unit 5 Achievement Test.

LEARNING OUTCOMES

> **Infer probability**
> **Take notes on supporting details**
> **Use context clues to understand vocabulary**

> **Use *because* and *even though***
> **Choose effective supporting details**
> **Write an opinion essay**

Go to **MyEnglishLab** to check what you know.

What Is Ecotourism?

1 FOCUS ON THE TOPIC

1. More and more people are traveling to Antarctica. What are some reasons people choose to travel to a place like Antarctica?

2. What is ecotourism? What do ecology[1] and tourism have in common?

3. What are some ways that natural places such as Antarctica can be damaged by tourists?

---

[1] **ecology:** the way in which plants, animals, and people are related to each other and to their environment, or the study of this

READING ONE | Tourists in a Fragile Land

VOCABULARY

1 Study the words and their definitions.

1. **coast:** the land next to the ocean

2. **consequence:** something that happens as a result of a particular action or situation

3. **fragile:** easily broken, damaged, or ruined

4. **harsh:** difficult to live in and very uncomfortable

5. **inhabit:** to live in an area or a place

6. **landscape:** the way an area of land looks

7. **preserve:** to save something or someone from being harmed or destroyed

8. **remote:** far away from towns and cities

9. **research:** serious study of a subject, especially in order to discover new facts or test new ideas

10. **tourist:** someone who is traveling or visiting a place for pleasure

11. **vast:** extremely large

2 How much do you know about Antarctica? Take this quiz—just for fun! Circle the answer you think is best. Pay special attention to the boldfaced words.

1. About _____ of Antarctica's **vast** land is covered with ice.

   a. 25 percent

   b. 50 percent

   c. 75 percent

   d. 98 percent

2. While Antarctica's **landscape** appears cold and snowy, the land of Antarctica is actually a _____ .

   a. desert

   b. forest

   c. jungle

   d. plain

3. The coldest temperature of the **harsh** Antarctic winter is approximately _____ .

   a. −35°C

   b. −50°C

   c. −90°C

   d. −120°C

4. Antarctica is **inhabited** by penguins and other animals, including _____ .

   a. bears

   b. seals

   c. eagles

   d. snow leopards

5. In _____ , a group of explorers led by Roald Amundsen became the first people to reach the **remote** South Pole.

   a. 1890

   b. 1911

   c. 1920

   d. 1952

6. The number of **tourists** visiting Antarctica increased from 4,698 in 1991 to approximately _____ in 2017.

   a. 8,000

   b. 10,000

   c. 18,000

   d. 45,000

7. In _____ , 12 countries signed the Antarctic Treaty to **preserve** the continent for scientific research.

   a. 1959

   b. 1978

   c. 1990

   d. 2002

8. In _____ , Emilio Palma was the first person born in Antarctica; his parents were living on the **coast** of Hope Bay.

   a. 1878

   b. 1950

   c. 1978

   d. 2006

9. Antarctica is colder than the Arctic as a **consequence** of its elevation—most of the continent is more than _____ above sea level.

   a. ½ kilometer

   b. 2 kilometers

   c. 10 kilometers

   d. 50 kilometers

10. In 2017, Ben Saunders walked through the **fragile** environment of Antarctica, trying to cross it alone. He had to quit after _____ days.

    a. 10

    b. 36

    c. 52

    d. 100

Answer Key: 1. d, 2. a, 3. c, 4. b, 5. b, 6. d, 7. a, 8. c, 9. b, 10. c

⬆ Go to the **Pearson Practice English App** or **My**English**Lab** for more vocabulary practice.

PREVIEW

Read the first paragraph of an opinion essay about tourism in Antarctica, written by a scientist who works there. Predict and write reasons why the scientist says, "I feel Antarctica should be closed to tourists."

1. _____

2. _____

3. _____

Read the opinion essay about Antarctica. Create a chart like the one below to take notes. On the left, put the main ideas. On the right, put the details.

TAKE NOTES

Main Ideas	Details
Scientist in Antarctica	studying ice
Ant. -- should be closed to tourists	oldest ice in world
	meteorologists—ozone hole, global warming
Ant. --- center of research	

Go to **MyEnglishLab** to view example notes.

Tourists in a Fragile Land

1 As a scientist working in Antarctica, I spend most of my time in the lab studying ice. I am trying to find out the age of Antarctic ice. All we know for certain is that it is the oldest ice in the world. The more we understand it, the more we will understand the changing weather of the Earth. Today, as with an increasing number of days, I had to leave my work to greet a group of **tourists** who were taking a vacation on this continent of ice. And even though I can appreciate their desire to experience this **vast** and beautiful **landscape**, I feel Antarctica should be closed to tourists.

2 Because Antarctica is the center of important scientific **research**, it must be **preserved** for this purpose. Meteorologists are now looking at the effects of the ozone hole[1] that was discovered above Antarctica in 1984. They are also trying to understand climate change[2]. If the Earth's temperature continues to increase, the health and safety of every living thing on the planet will be affected. Astronomers have a unique view of space and are able to see it very clearly from Antarctica. Biologists have a chance to learn more about the animals that **inhabit** the **coast** of this frozen land. Botanists study the plant life to understand

---

[1] **ozone hole:** a hole in the layer of gases that protect the Earth from the bad effects of the sun
[2] **climate change:** a general increase in world temperatures caused by increased amounts of carbon dioxide around the Earth

how it can live in such a **harsh** environment, and geologists study the Earth to learn more about how it was formed. There are even psychologists who study how people behave when they live and work together in such a **remote** location.

3 Tourists in Antarctica can damage scientific research and hurt the environment by mistake. First, many tourists come here. When they visit our labs, they take our attention away from research. Our work is difficult, and some of our projects can be damaged by such simple mistakes as opening the wrong door or bumping into a small piece of equipment. In addition, tourists in Antarctica can also hurt the environment. Members of Greenpeace, one of the world's leading environmental organizations, complain that tourists leave trash on beaches and disturb the plants and animals. In a place as frozen as Antarctica, it can take 100 years for a plant to grow back. Tourists can also easily damage penguin eggs. Oil spills are another problem caused by tourism because they kill penguins and can also destroy scientific projects.

4 The need to protect Antarctica from tourists becomes even greater when we consider the fact that it is not a country, so there is no government here. The entire continent is set aside as a scientific preserve. So, who is making sure that the penguins, plants, and

sea are safe? No one is responsible. In fact, we scientists are only temporary visitors ourselves. It is true that the number of tourists who visit Antarctica each year is small compared to the number of those who visit other places. However, these other places are inhabited by local residents and controlled by local governments. They have an interest in protecting their natural environments. Who is concerned about the environment of Antarctica? The scientists, to be sure, but not necessarily the tour companies that make money from sending people south.

5 If we don't protect Antarctica from tourism, there may be serious **consequences** for us all. We might lose the results of scientific research projects. It's possible that this information could teach us something important about the causes and effects of climate change. Some **fragile** plants and animals might die and disappear forever. This could damage the balance of animal and plant life in Antarctica. We know from past experience that when things get unbalanced, harmful changes can occur. Clearly, Antarctica should remain a place for careful and controlled scientific research. We cannot allow tourism to bring possible danger to the Earth. The only way to protect this fragile and important part of the planet is to stop tourists from traveling to Antarctica.

MAIN IDEAS

The body of the essay (paragraphs 2, 3, 4), gives three main reasons why Antarctica should be closed to tourists. Number the reasons in the order in which they appear. Use your notes to help you.

_____ There is no government to protect Antarctica.

_____ Tourists can damage scientific research that can be conducted only in Antarctica.

_____ Tourists can damage Antarctica's environment.

DETAILS

1 **These statements are false or incomplete. Rewrite them with information from Reading One so they are true and complete. Use your notes to help you.**

1. The writer of the essay knows the age of Antarctic ice.

   The writer of the essay is trying to find out the age of Antarctic ice.

2. The writer wants Antarctica to be closed.

   _____

3. Psychologists study how people behave when they get lost in Antarctica.

   _____

4. Oil spills in Antarctica have killed scientists.

   _____

5. When tourists visit labs, they help scientists focus on research.

   _____

6. If we don't protect Antarctica from tourism, there will be serious consequences for a few scientists.

   _____

7. We know from past experience that when things get balanced, harmful changes can occur.

   _____

2 **Look at your notes and your answers in Preview. How did they help you to understand the article?**

Inferring Probability

An **inference** is an **educated guess** about something that is **not directly stated** in a text. Writers sometimes **suggest whether something** is likely or unlikely without directly stating it.

Look at the example and read the explanation.

> "Because Antarctica is the center for important scientific research, it must be preserved for this purpose." *(paragraph 2)*

We will find out about different types of scientists that work in Antarctica. Choose the best answer.

a. likely

b. unlikely

*(The best answer is **a**.)*

In **paragraph 2,** the author tells us that Antarctica should be preserved because it is very important for scientific research. Since this is the topic sentence of the paragraph, we can guess that the paragraph will contain more information about different types of scientists working in Antarctica.

After reading the text closely, we can **infer** that it is **likely** that we will find out about different types of scientists that work in Antarctica.

1 **Read the statements. Choose the best answer to indicate how likely or unlikely it is. Look at the paragraphs in parentheses.**

    1. Tourists make living in Antarctica stressful. *(paragraph 3)*

       a. likely   b. unlikely

    2. For Greenpeace, Antarctica is one of the most important areas in the world. *(paragraph 3)*

       a. likely   b. unlikely

    3. Antarctica will form a government. *(paragraph 4)*

       a. likely   b. unlikely

    4. Scientists enjoy tourists. *(paragraph 5)*

       a. likely   b. unlikely

2 **Now discuss your answers with a partner. Point out words, phrases, or statements that helped you find the answers.**

Work in small groups. Choose one of the questions. Discuss your ideas. Then choose one person in your group to report the ideas to the class.

USE YOUR NOTES

Use your notes to support your answers with information from the reading.

1. Do you agree with the scientist's opinions about closing Antarctica to tourists? Explain.

2. Why is it so difficult to protect Antarctica? How do you think it should be protected?

3. Which types of scientists are studying Antarctica? Which type of study do you think is the most important? Why?

◐ Go to **MyEnglishLab** to give your opinion about another question.

READING TWO | A Travel Journal

PREVIEW

1 Look at the photos below and the title on the next page. Read the first paragraph. Write two questions that you think will be answered in this reading.

_____

_____

2 Look at the boldfaced words in the reading. Which words do you know the meaning of?

READ

1 Read these entries from the journal of a tourist who traveled to Antarctica. As you read, guess the meanings of words that are new to you. Remember to take notes on main ideas and details.

2 After you finish reading, compare your notes on main ideas and details with a partner's. How can you improve your notes next time?

◐ Go to the **Pearson Practice English App** or **MyEnglishLab** for more vocabulary practice.

A TRAVEL JOURNAL

Chile, South America
February 16
1 The sunlight was shining so brightly as our plane flew over the snow-covered Andes Mountains, which seemed to go on forever.

Cape Horn
February 18
2 We spent the morning at a small church named Star of the Sea. This is a quiet place where visitors are invited to remember the sailors from all over the world who died here. They were all trying to sail around the southern part of South America, and many of them lost their lives at sea.

Drake Passage—aboard the tour ship *Explorer*
February 19
3 We were welcomed today by the captain and crew. They gave us warm Antarctic jackets and introduced themselves to us. Sea birds followed the ship closely, sailing in the cold wind. As we headed south, we saw a pink ship in the distance. Our captain explained that it was not a ship but an iceberg[1]—the first one of our trip.

Deception Island, Antarctica
February 21
4 We landed on Baily Head, where thousands and thousands of penguins greeted us. The crew gave us a set of rules to follow to **protect** the environment. Mark, one of the scientists on our ship, asked us to bring him any trash that we find. He is studying the amount of trash created by tourists in Antarctica each year.

5 Tonight we'll listen to Christina, another scientist. She will explain the plant and animal life to us. Then she will give us a list of interesting websites that we can visit to learn more about Antarctica.

6 The more I see of this remote place, the more I want to learn.

Cuverville Island, Antarctica
February 23
7 We awakened this morning to the noisy sound of penguins. They're loud! We met a team of biologists living in tents. They are studying the effect of tourists on baby penguins. When our captain invited the biologists to come on board for a hot shower, they joined us immediately. Then we cruised through the icebergs, which appeared in unbelievable shapes and sizes, as the sun was sinking in the sky. They seemed to be works of art by an ice sculptor[2].

Paradise Bay, Antarctica
February 25
8 Today, we reached the mainland of the **continent**. Our guide today was Stephanie, who helped us walk through snow to a point about 500 feet above sea level. When we reached the top, we laughed like children because it was so much fun to be up there. Later, we **explored** a glacier[3] in motorized rubber boats. The ice was as thick as the crushed ice in a soft drink, but we pushed through it.

Detaille Island, Antarctica
February 28
9 Because we wanted to celebrate crossing the Antarctic Circle, we drank some champagne today. Not many visitors come this far south! Mark explained an interesting **characteristic** of the ice down here. It is blue because it catches all the colors of the rainbow except for blue. I have always thought of Antarctica as nothing but white. But now I see a clear blue light shining through the mountains of ice all around us, and I have no words to describe the beauty of this landscape.

10 Our ship passed a huge field of frozen sea. Mark invited us to come out and play. We weren't sure at first, but when we felt how solid it was, we jumped and ran. All around us were mountains and glaciers that no one has ever explored. It amazed me to think that no human hand or foot has ever touched them; only a few human eyes have seen them.

11 Even though it will be hard to describe, I will try to explain this amazing experience to my friends at home. We all felt sad today when we realized that our ship was heading north. We really aren't ready to leave Antarctica, a unique world.

---

[1] **iceberg:** an extremely large piece of ice floating in the sea

[2] **sculptor:** an artist who makes objects from clay, wood, metal, ice, etc.

[3] **glacier:** a large area of ice that moves slowly over an area of land

Taking Notes on Supporting Details

When you take notes, write details that support main ideas. This will help you to understand how information is organized in a reading. It will also help you to prepare for tests and other assignments. Look at the example and notice how the details support the idea that Antarctica is very interesting.

Antarctica is a very interesting place to visit.

a) Supporting detail: ice

- iceberg looks like a pink ship
- icebergs have unbelievable shapes and sizes
- glacier ice: like crushed ice in a soft drink
- color of ice = blue

b) Supporting details: animals and nature

- thousands of noisy penguins
- a frozen sea

1 Add more details to support the main ideas. Write details next to each letter.

1. There are rules that tourists can follow in Antarctica.

   a. _____

2. Tourists can support and help scientists.

   a. _____

   b. _____

3. Tourists can learn and teach others about Antarctica.

   a. _____

   b. _____

   c. _____

2 Look at Reading Two again. Mark the information you think is most important.

Go to **MyEnglishLab** for more note-taking practice.

COMPREHENSION

1 **Answer the questions. Use your notes from Reading Two to help you. Discuss your answers with a partner.**

1. How did the writer feel about her trip? What adjectives describe her emotions?

2. What opinion does the writer have about tourism in Antarctica? How do you know?

2 **Review the boldfaced words from the reading with a partner. Use a dictionary or ask your teacher for any meanings you still do not know.**

READING SKILL

1 **Read paragraph 3 of Reading Two again. What is the meaning of the word *captain*? What information before or after this word helps you to understand what it means?**

Using Context Clues to Understand Vocabulary

Good readers use context clues to understand new vocabulary in a text. Context clues are other words or phrases that help you figure out the meaning of a word you don't know. Context clues can come before or after the word.

Look at the example and read the explanation:

> "We were welcomed today by the captain and crew. . . . Our captain explained that it was not a ship but an iceberg—the first one of our trip." *(paragraph 3)*

These sentences come after the subheading "Drake Passage—aboard the tour ship *Explorer*." This subheading contains a word that you might already know: *ship*. If you know that a ship is a boat, you could guess that a captain is someone who leads a ship. If you notice that the captain explained something to others, you might also understand that he or she is an important person, or leader. Also, pay attention to words that are repeated more than once. In paragraph 3, *captain* is repeated twice. This gives you more context clues to use.

Using context clues helps you understand a passage more quickly and easily.

2 **Work with a partner to answer questions about Reading Two. Guess the meanings of the words by using context clues.**

1. Read paragraph 7. What is the meaning of *cruised*?

   a. moved along slowly
   b. moved along quickly

2. Read paragraph 8. What is the meaning of *crushed*?

   a. something is very cold
   b. something is broken into pieces

3. Read paragraph 8. What is the meaning of *guide*?

   a. a person who takes tourists to new places
   b. a website giving tourists advice

4. Read paragraph 10. What is the meaning of *solid*?

   a. soft with holes
   b. hard with no holes

🅠 Go to **MyEnglishLab** for more skill practice.

ORGANIZE

USE YOUR NOTES

Review your notes from Reading One and Two. Use the information in your notes to complete the exercise.

Reading One (R1) shares a scientist's opinion on the negative effects of tourism in Antarctica. Reading Two (R2) shares the perspective of a tourist and shows that it is possible for tourists to have a positive effect in Antarctica. Write S next to statements that give the viewpoint of a scientist and T next to statements that give the viewpoint of a tourist.

1. The Antarctic environment must be preserved for research. _____

2. We cannot control the behavior of tourists. _____

3. Tourists can actually help scientists with their experiments. _____

4. Tourists are interested in learning about Antarctica. _____

5. Tourists take scientists away from their research, can damage scientific projects, and hurt the environment. _____

6. Tourists can follow rules made by scientists. _____

7. As tourists learn about Antarctica and return home to tell their friends and families about its importance, they may want to help preserve the environment of Antarctica. _____

8. Tourists don't care about Antarctica. _____

SYNTHESIZE

Use information from Organize to complete the summary of both opinions. Change the grammar and syntax from the statements in Organize as needed.

There is strong disagreement about the question of allowing tourists to visit Antarctica.

Because many tourists _____ , they will be happy to learn from guides
.   1.

and scientists who can teach them about this unique world. Tourists can also participate

_____ . For example, they can help scientists collect trash to study.
.   2.

Others may want to help preserve Antarctica's environment as they learn about its importance

from tourists who _____ . However, many scientists strongly believe that
.   3.

Antarctica should be closed to all visitors. There may be damage to the environment because

_____ . Tourists might also harm _____ and make
.   4.   5.

it hard for scientists to focus on _____ . Even though some tourists may
.   6.

care about Antarctica, _____ . They are just trying to have fun in a remote
.   7.

location. For these reasons, scientists believe we must _____ .
.   8.

🔊 Go to **MyEnglishLab** to check what you learned.

VOCABULARY

REVIEW

Work in a small group. Match the adjectives in the box with the nouns from Reading One and Reading Two surrounding them. List as many possible combinations as you can think of.

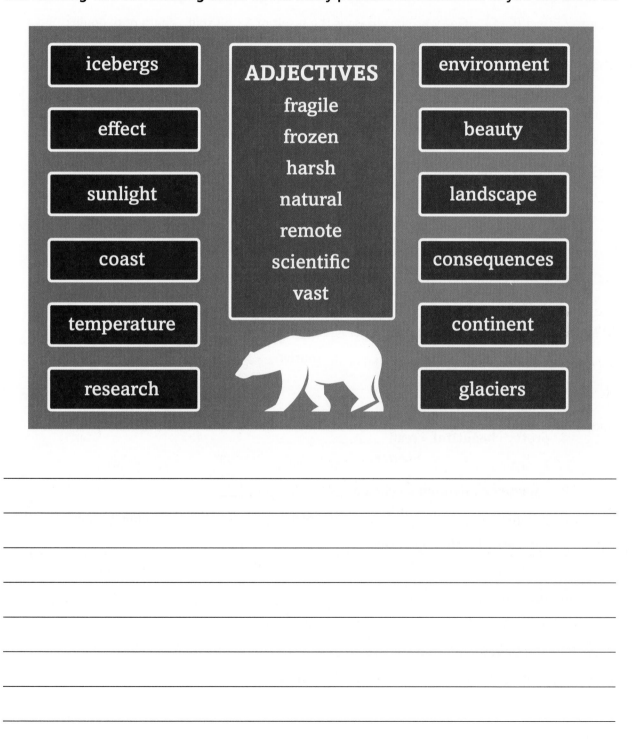

icebergs

effect

sunlight

coast

temperature

research

ADJECTIVES
fragile
frozen
harsh
natural
remote
scientific
vast

environment

beauty

landscape

consequences

continent

glaciers

_____

_____

_____

_____

_____

_____

_____

_____

EXPAND

Read the chart. Notice how the categories, definitions, and examples relate to one another. Then complete the exercise by analyzing the relationships between the vocabulary words. First, choose the word that best completes each comparison. Be sure that the second pair of words has a similar relationship to the first pair. Second, label each comparison with the letter of the correct category.

CATEGORY	DEFINITION	EXAMPLE
Synonym (S)	The words have a similar meaning.	work : job
Antonym (A)	The words have opposite meanings.	harsh : gentle
Cause / Effect (C / E)	One word or phrase is the result of another word or phrase.	oil spill : death of penguins
Degree (D)	One word has a stronger meaning than the other.	damaged : destroyed

_____ 1. **unique : rare** = huge : _____

      a. fragile   b. remote   c. vast

_____ 2. **heavy rain : flood** = vast ice fields : _____

      a. cooler temperature   b. ozone layer   c. climate change

_____ 3. **protected : preserved** = surprising : _____

      a. temporary   b. amazing   c. fragile

_____ 4. **harsh : comfortable** = inland : _____

      a. coast   b. global   c. ocean

_____ 5. **consequence : effect** = traveler : _____

      a. climate   b. tourist   c. researcher

_____ 6. **project : work** = far : _____

      a. harsh   b. remote   c. vast

_____ 7. **pretty : beautiful** = read : _____

      a. scan   b. predict   c. research

_____ 8. **careful : controlled** = delicate : _____

      a. quiet   b. fragile   c. unbelievable

_____ 9. **tourists : trash** = scientists : _____

      a. research   b. environment   c. continents

_____ 10. **inhabit : live** = beautiful : _____

      a. scenic   b. uncrowded   c. pleasant

_____ 11. **comfortable : harsh** = cold : _____

      a. hot   b. frozen   c. icy

CREATE

APPLY Think of a place of natural beauty that you have visited. Write five sentences to describe this place, using the words in the box. You may change the form of the words.

environment	inhabit	landscape	protect	tourists

Go to the **Pearson Practice English App** or **MyEnglishLab** for more vocabulary practice.

GRAMMAR FOR WRITING

1 Look at the sentences. What do they mean?

- Because Antarctica is the center of important scientific research, it must be preserved.

- Even though I can appreciate tourists' desire to experience this beautiful landscape, I feel Antarctica should be closed to them.

Because and *Even Though*

1. *Because* gives a **reason**.	Main Clause ⸻ Dependent Clause Antarctica must be preserved *because* it is the center of important scientific research. Dependent Clause ⸻ Main Clause *Because* Antarctica is beautiful, tourists enjoy it.
2. *Even though* explains an **unexpected result**. It can also express a **contrast,** or difference. (*Although* can be used in a similar way.)	Main Clause Some scientists in Antarctica do not find answers to Dependent Clause their questions *even though* they work very hard. Dependent Clause *Even though* some people want to visit Antarctica, Main Clause others do not.

3. Each sentence above has a **main clause** and a **dependent clause.** (A main clause can stand alone. A dependent clause cannot.)

   The **dependent clauses** begin with *because* or *even though*. Always use a **comma** after the dependent clause when it begins the sentence.

2 Combine each pair of sentences using *because* or *even though*. Add a comma when the dependent clause comes before the main clause. For questions 2–4, put the dependent clause first. For questions 5–7, put the main clause first.

1. I had to interrupt my research and greet tourists. I was very busy.

   Even though I was very busy, I had to interrupt my research and greet tourists.

2. I understand why tourists want to see Antarctica. They shouldn't be allowed to visit.

   _____

3. The Earth's temperature is rising. Meteorologists are worried.

   _____

4. Antarctica's unique environment is in danger. There is no government to help preserve it.

   _____

5. Tourists enjoy the beauty of Antarctica. They sometimes damage the environment.

   _____

6. Scientists are interested in protecting Antarctica's natural environment. Tour companies are not.

   _____

7. We had an amazing time on this remote continent. It was difficult to travel in such a harsh environment.

   _____

3 **APPLY** Use your own ideas to complete the sentences using *because* or *even though*. Choose the appropriate verb form.

1. I **would / wouldn't** like to visit Antarctica _____

   _____ .

2. _____ ,

   tourism **should / shouldn't** be allowed in Antarctica.

3. Antarctica **should / shouldn't** be closed to tourists _____

   _____ .

4. I **would / wouldn't** like to be a scientist in Antarctica _____

   _____ .

🡒 Go to the **Pearson Practice English App** or **MyEnglishLab** for more grammar practice. Check what you learned in **MyEnglishLab**.

FINAL WRITING TASK: An Opinion Essay 🔍 **APPLY**

In this unit, you read opinions about tourists visiting Antarctica, a remote place that has a fragile environment. What is your opinion about tourism there?

You are going to *write an opinion essay about whether or not tourists should be allowed to explore other remote places that have fragile environments.* You will give reasons why these places should be open or closed to tourism. Use the vocabulary and grammar from the unit.

For an alternative writing topic, see page 145.

PREPARE TO WRITE: Listing

1 Listing is a technique that helps writers gather ideas. You can list ideas from readings as well as your own ideas. Look back at the opinions in Organize, page 136. Think about how these opinions relate to the places you will write about in your essay. Make a list of opinions from the chart that will help you write. Add your own opinions to the list. When you are finished, decide which opinions are the best for your essay.

1. _____

2. _____

3. _____

4. _____

5. _____

6. _____

2 Share your list with a partner. Do you have different opinions? Discuss them.

WRITE

Writing an Opinion Essay

An **essay** is a piece of nonfiction writing that has more than one or two paragraphs and is organized around a central idea. An **opinion essay** expresses an opinion about something. There are three important parts of a good opinion essay:

Introductory Paragraph

- It introduces your topic.
- It includes a thesis statement that states the main idea of the essay (your opinion). The thesis statement is usually the last sentence in the paragraph.

Body (at least one paragraph)

- Each paragraph of the body starts with a topic sentence that states a reason for your opinion.
- The topic sentence is followed by details that support the reason for your opinion. These supporting details can be facts, examples, or explanations.
  - It can take 100 years for a plant to grow back in Antarctica. (fact)
  - Astronomers and biologists are two types of scientists who work in Antarctica. (example)
  - Antarctica has no government, which means that no one is making sure that the penguins, plants, and sea are safe. (explanation)

Concluding Paragraph

- It restates the main idea expressed in your thesis statement.

1 Complete the tasks for Reading One.

1. Look at the introductory paragraph. Find the thesis statement. Write it here.

   _____

2. Underline the topic sentence of each body paragraph.

3. In paragraphs 2, 3, and 4, what types of supporting details are used (facts, examples, or explanations)?

   Paragraph 2: _____

   Paragraph 3: _____

   Paragraph 4: _____

4. Find the concluding sentence that restates the main idea. Write it here.

   _____

2 You are going to write an opinion essay about whether or not tourists should be allowed to explore other remote places that have fragile environments. Your essay will have four paragraphs: an introductory paragraph, two body paragraphs, and a concluding paragraph. In the body, give reasons to support your opinion and details to support your reasons. Use *because* and *even though* to help explain your reasons for your opinion. Plan your first draft by completing the outline.

   I. Introductory Paragraph:

     Thesis Statement (your opinion about tourism):

     _____

  II. Body Paragraph:

     Topic Sentence (one reason for your opinion):

     _____

     Supporting Details (facts, examples, or explanations):

     _____

 III. Body Paragraph:

     Topic Sentence (one reason for your opinion):

     _____

     Supporting Details (facts, examples, or explanations):

     _____

  IV. Concluding Paragraph:

     Restatement of thesis (restate your opinion about tourism):

     _____

3 Look at your list from Prepare to Write on page 141. Use your list and your outline to write the first draft of your essay.

- Make sure your essay has four paragraphs: an introductory paragraph, two body paragraphs, and a concluding paragraph.

- Your body paragraphs should give reasons to support your opinion and details to support your reasons.

- Use *because* to explain reasons and *even though* to describe unexpected results.

REVISE: Choosing Effective Supporting Details

1 Read the sentence about a tourist's visit to Antarctica. Underline the details that describe the sunlight and the Andes Mountains.

The sunlight was shining so brightly as our plane flew over the snow-covered Andes Mountains, which seemed to go on forever.

Effective Supporting Details

Good writers give strong reasons for their opinions. They choose effective supporting details to help the reader understand their reasons. Effective supporting details may include facts, examples, or explanations.

Look at Sentence 1:

1. Our work is difficult, and some of our projects can be damaged by such simple mistakes as opening the wrong door or bumping into a small piece of equipment.

   Underline two examples of simple mistakes. In the writer's opinion, why are they a problem?

Look at Sentence 2:

2. When we reached the top, which was 500 miles above sea level, we laughed like children because we were having so much fun up there.

   Underline a fact about the place they reached. Underline the explanation of why tourists laughed.

2 Now read a paragraph about tourism on Cape Cod. There are three supporting details that are weak and need to be revised. Find and underline the supporting details in the body paragraph. Label them (a), (b), and (c). The first one has been done for you.

My family lives on Cape Cod in Massachusetts. Cape Cod is a

long piece of land that goes out into the Atlantic Ocean. There

are beaches on two sides. It is a beautiful place, but there is too

much tourism. I think Cape Cod should limit the number of

tourists who visit every summer. Tourism is hurting Cape Cod

in several ways. First, there are not many good jobs for people on Cape Cod. The jobs don't pay well. (a)

In addition, living on Cape Cod during the summer is very expensive. Everything is expensive. Finally,

tourists hurt the environment. There are too many people. I would like to live on Cape Cod for the

rest of my life. However, I will have to leave if so many tourists visit each summer. That's why I

believe that tourism is not good for Cape Cod.

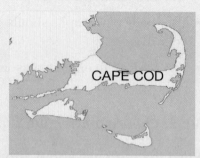

CAPE COD

3 The details above are weak because they do not provide facts, examples, or explanations to support the reasons for the writer's opinion. They are too general. The supporting details below are stronger because they include more specific information. Decide which details should replace those you underlined in the paragraph in Exercise Two. Write the correct letter next to each detail.

_____ 1. About 6 million people visit Cape Cod each year. These people bring their cars, so there is a lot of traffic. They crowd the beaches and pollute the ocean.

_____ 2. Most jobs are in hotels, restaurants, or souvenir shops. These jobs have low pay and require very hard work.

_____ 3. The cost of living is higher for both tourists and people who live in the Cape year-round. The prices of gas, groceries, and entertainment all increase.

4 What kinds of supporting details did you add: facts, examples, or explanations? Do you think the details are effective? Why or why not?

5 Now go back to the first draft of your essay.

- Make sure your supporting details are effective. They should include facts, examples, and explanations that make the ideas clear. Make revisions if needed.

- Try to use the grammar and some of the vocabulary from the unit.

Go to **MyEnglishLab** for more skill practice.

EDIT: Writing the Final Draft

APPLY Write the final draft of your paragraph and submit it to your teacher. Carefully edit it for grammatical and mechanical errors, such as spelling, capitalization, and punctuation. Consider how to apply the vocabulary, grammar, and writing skills from the unit. Use the checklist to help you.

FINAL DRAFT CHECKLIST

☐ Does your essay express your opinion about allowing tourism in a remote and fragile place?

☐ Does it contain an introductory paragraph, two body paragraphs, and a concluding paragraph?

☐ Does the introductory paragraph contain a thesis statement stating the main idea of the essay (your opinion)?

☐ Does each body paragraph contain a topic sentence stating the main idea of the paragraph (a reason for your opinion)?

☐ Does each body paragraph contain at least two details supporting the reason for your opinion?

☐ Are the details facts, examples, or explanations?

☐ Does the concluding paragraph restate the main idea expressed in the thesis statement?

☐ Are the *because* and *even though* clauses used correctly?

☐ Do these clauses have the correct punctuation?

☐ Do you use new vocabulary from the unit?

ALTERNATIVE WRITING TOPIC

APPLY With all the human suffering in the world, is it still important to protect plants and animals? Why? Write an essay giving your opinion about this topic. Use the grammar and vocabulary from the unit.

CHECK WHAT YOU'VE LEARNED

Check (✔) the outcomes you've met and vocabulary you've learned. Put an X next to the skills and vocabulary you still need to practice.

Learning Outcomes

☐ **Infer probability**

☐ **Take notes on supporting details**

☐ **Use context clues to understand vocabulary**

☐ **Use *because* and *even though***

☐ **Choose effective supporting details**

☐ **Write an opinion essay**

Vocabulary

☐ **characteristic**

☐ **coast**

☐ **consequence** AWL

☐ **continent**

☐ **explore**

☐ **fragile**

☐ **harsh**

☐ **inhabit**

☐ **landscape**

☐ **preserve**

☐ **protect**

☐ **remote**

☐ **research (n.)** AWL

☐ **tourist**

☐ **vast**

🔵 Go to **MyEnglishLab** to watch a video about ecotourism, access the Unit Project, and take the Unit 6 Achievement Test.

LEARNING OUTCOMES

> Infer both sides of a debate
> Take notes with an outline
> Identify key information in charts

> Use adverb clauses of concession
> Use sentence variety
> Write an opinion essay

🔊 Go to **MyEnglishLab** to check what you know.

Capital Punishment

1 FOCUS ON THE TOPIC

1. Think about different crimes, from minor (not a serious problem) to severe (a very serious problem). What are some different punishments for these crimes?

2. Capital punishment (the death penalty) means taking the life of someone who has committed a crime. What are some countries you know of that practice capital punishment?

3. Do you agree with capital punishment? If so, for what kind of crimes? If you disagree with capital punishment, explain your reasons.

READING ONE | Life in Prison Is Still Life: Why Should a Killer Live? / Why Do We Kill People to Show That Killing People Is Wrong?

VOCABULARY

1 Read the fact sheet about capital punishment. Pay attention to the boldfaced words.

FACT SHEET

- Charles Manson led a group of **murderers** who shocked the United States with terrible killings. Even though Manson spent his life in prison, the lawyer who fought against him said that such murderers are a danger to everyone and cannot be allowed to live.

- In 2007, 310 prisoners in Italy asked their president to give them the death penalty because they were suffering in prison. They felt that capital punishment is less **cruel** because it prevents the pain of prison life.

- Some prisoners do not receive **justice**. In prison, they are sometimes killed for **revenge**—because of things they have done before. Here, the prisoners become victims and are not shown **forgiveness**.

- In 2017, Guinea stopped using the death penalty for all crimes, giving everyone, including murderers, the legal **right** to live.

- In 2016, when the United Nations recommended that all countries stop using the death penalty, India chose to keep it. This indicates a very strong feeling that murderers and other dangerous people are not safe for **society**.

- Rwanda stopped using the death penalty in 2007. This African country, which has experienced a great deal of violence, wanted to show the world that its people have **respect** for the right to life, even for murderers.

- In 2018, Japan's Justice Minister supported the execution[1] of a leader whose group poisoned over 6,000 people on the Tokyo subway system. Twenty-seven of these people died, and the rest were very sick. Studies show that a majority of people in Japan agree with capital punishment in such extreme cases.

- In 2017, Mongolia **abolished** the death penalty. The new law says that no one can be executed for any crime.

- Since 1973, in the United States, there have been 163 prisoners sentenced to death who were later found to be **innocent**. Unfortunately, 15 had already been executed.

- Son of Sam was a **violent** killer who murdered six people and badly hurt nine others. He made an announcement that he would kill again. After he said this, many Americans were angry and supported the death penalty.

- In 2017, 2,591 people who were found **guilty** of murder and other crimes were sentenced to death in 53 countries.

[1] **execution:** the act of killing someone legally as punishment

2 Match the words on the left with the definitions on the right.

_____ 1. murderers

_____ 2. cruel

_____ 3. justice

_____ 4. revenge

_____ 5. forgiveness

_____ 6. right

_____ 7. respect

_____ 8. abolished

_____ 9. society

_____ 10. innocent

_____ 11. violent

_____ 12. guilty

a. something you do in order to punish someone who has harmed or offended you

b. an attitude of regarding something or someone as important, so that you are careful not to harm them

c. having done something that is a crime

d. officially ended a law or system

e. a particular large group of people who share laws, organizations, customs, etc.

f. the act of not blaming someone or being angry with them

g. people who kill others

h. not guilty of a crime

i. something you are allowed to do legally, morally, or officially

j. involving actions that are intended to injure or kill people by hitting them, shooting them, etc.

k. making someone suffer or feel unhappy

l. fairness in the way people are treated

Go to the **Pearson Practice English App** or **MyEnglishLab** for more vocabulary practice.

PREVIEW

A newspaper editorial gives the writer's opinion about a topic. An editorial begins with a headline, or title, that helps us know the author's opinion. Look at the titles of the two editorials. What do you think is the opinion of each editorial? Choose the correct answer. Compare your answer with a partner's.

Editorial 1: Life in Prison Is Still Life: Why Should a Killer Live?

a. This editorial agrees with capital punishment.

b. This editorial disagrees with capital punishment.

Editorial 2: Why Do We Kill People to Show That Killing People Is Wrong?

a. This editorial agrees with capital punishment.

b. This editorial disagrees with capital punishment.

READ

Read the two editorials about capital on the next two pages. Create charts like the one below to take notes. On the left, put the main ideas. On the right, put the details.

TAKE NOTES: Editorial 1

Main Ideas	Details
Strong Reasons for CP	
1. Justice	unjust—not fair for murderers to live while victims die

TAKE NOTES: Editorial 2

Main Ideas	Details
Reasons for Prison, not CP	
1. Execution of innocent	possible = innocent person will die
	b/c government can't decide perfectly, justice system not perfect

Go to **MyEnglishLab** to view example notes.

Life in Prison Is Still Life: Why Should a Killer Live?

1 While many people around the world disagree with capital punishment, there are many others who support it. In the United States, 60 percent of Americans agree with capital punishment as a way of keeping society safe and just. In 58 other countries, including Japan and Singapore, many believe that a **murderer** should give up all rights, including the right to life. On the other hand, some worry that **innocent** people may be killed by mistake, and others believe that no one has the right to take a life, not even the government. Despite the fact that no society can manage its system of capital punishment perfectly, there are strong reasons why the death penalty should be used against murderers in many cases.

2 The first reason is that capital punishment is the best way to keep **justice** at the center of our **society**. Murder is a terrible injustice. Victims of murder lose their lives—which, unlike stolen money or property, can never be replaced. The victims' hopes and plans have ended permanently, and the pleasures they enjoyed in life have been destroyed. They will never see their loved ones again. But without capital punishment, murderers are allowed to stay alive and even to enjoy their lives in some ways. This is completely unjust because they have ended the lives of people who did not want to die.

3 Another reason for capital punishment is that the tax money of citizens, including taxes paid by victims' families, should not be used to support the life of a murderer. In the state of California, it costs nearly $90,000 a year to keep each killer alive in prison. Today there are murderers in prisons all over the world. Most of them would rather spend their lives in prison than die. Even in prison, there are small pleasures that one can enjoy every day: the feeling of warm sunshine, the taste of a hot meal, the comfort of sleep. The lifestyle in prison is not always harsh; many prisoners can continue their education, play sports, enjoy movies, and receive visits. Because of these benefits, sometimes prisoners who have been released commit more crimes just so they can return to prison. According to the Bureau of Justice Statistics, more than 79 percent of released prisoners head back to prison within six years of their release. And why wouldn't they? Who wouldn't want to enjoy their **right** to free meals and shelter, all provided by taxpayers?

4 The final reason for keeping the death penalty is that it stops a person from killing again. Capital punishment is the only sure way of taking these killers away from society forever. Kenneth McDuff is an example of the worst kind of criminal—one who has no **respect** for life. He murdered three people and spent 20 years in prison. When he was released from prison, he killed nine more people. Another example is Timothy McVeigh. He killed 168 people and injured more than 500 others in a terrorist attack against his own country. He built a bomb and used it to destroy a government building, which included a child care center where 19 children were killed. His execution, which was supported by 80 percent of Americans, is a clear example of how capital punishment is necessary in such extreme cases to keep society safe. It also sends a strong message to others who plan to kill: Be prepared to pay with your own life.

5 While there is always the chance that an innocent person could be given the death penalty by mistake, such cases are rare. Capital punishment is unfortunate but must be legal in cases of extreme violence. As Russian historian Aleksandr Solzhenitsyn said, "There are times when the government needs capital punishment in order to save society." Indeed, a society without justice is one where the rights of murderers are respected more than those of the innocent.

Why Do We Kill People to Show That Killing People Is Wrong?

1   There are times when murder is not committed because of cruelty. People may kill for other reasons, such as anger, misunderstanding, or fear. These feelings cause people to make mistakes all the time, and sometimes they can even lead someone to murder another person. This means that any one of us could commit murder because of feelings that are too strong to handle. For society, it is a serious mistake to take the life of someone who has killed because it teaches everyone that **forgiveness** is not an option. Despite the fact that murder is a terrible crime, there are several reasons why the death penalty should not be used.

2   The first reason is that innocent people might be executed by mistake. The government has the difficult job of deciding who is innocent and who is **guilty**, and this job cannot be done perfectly. If capital punishment is allowed, it is always possible that an innocent person will die. In the United States, many prisoners waiting to be executed have been found innocent. Since 1973, 151 prisoners who were waiting to be executed have been freed instead. They could have been the victims of a justice system that can never be perfect.

3   Another reason is that capital punishment does not stop the crime of murder. Though some people may be scared of the death penalty, there is no proof that it works better in preventing crime than any other punishment. In fact, it might even encourage some people to commit crimes. Even though some believe that the idea of being executed scares people and stops them from doing wrong, this is not actually true. In fact, crime rates are higher in American states that allow capital punishment, such as Texas and California. The United States government once followed the example of Germany, Britain, France, and developed nations that have **abolished** the death penalty. Sadly, it is now using a **cruel** and **violent** form of punishment that does not make society safer.

4   We should also stop using the death penalty because of the high cost, both financial and emotional. It costs the taxpayer millions of dollars more to execute a criminal than to imprison that criminal for life. Also, we cannot imagine the pain of family members who have been waiting for years for the government's decision to execute or not execute their loved ones. Execution does not always bring peace to the family members of victims. In 2016, *Psychology Today* reported a study showing that only 2.5 percent of victims' family members felt that execution brought them justice. On the other hand, 20 percent said that execution did nothing to bring back their loved ones or reduce the pain of losing them. Prison is a better form of punishment because it protects society and punishes criminals by taking away their freedom.

5   Most importantly, we should stop using capital punishment against our fellow humans because people can change, even people who have made terrible mistakes. Life in prison gives people the chance to improve themselves. Myuran Sukumaran is an example of someone who became a better person in prison. He created museum-quality paintings and helped other prisoners by starting an art school for them. After his execution, another artist said he was an example of how "bad people can become good people." His partner in crime, Andrew Chan, was also sent to prison, where he became a Christian pastor. Likewise, Jaturun Siripongs, who had murdered two liquor store employees, became a Buddhist monk while he was on death row. They found respect for life and never committed another crime. These changed men show that even though life in prison means losing freedom and not being able to do what you want, prisoners can still grow and create better lives.

6   While some people believe that **revenge** is necessary for justice, Indian leader Mahatma Gandhi taught that, "an eye for an eye leaves the whole world blind." The examples of prisoners who change show us that people can learn from mistakes. But a dead person learns nothing, and an executed person will never change. When a government uses capital punishment to kill its own citizens, it is expressing harmful revenge and murdering the hope of a better society.

MAIN IDEAS

The two editorials express different opinions about capital punishment.

Editorial 1 / Opinion A: Execution is a better form of punishment than life in prison.

Editorial 2 / Opinion B: Life in prison is a better form of punishment than execution.

Read the main ideas. Use your notes to determine if they are from Editorial 1 (A) or Editorial 2 (B). Write *A* or *B* on the line.

_____ 1. Execution may cause an innocent person to die.

_____ 2. Prisoners are able to enjoy life, and this is not fair.

_____ 3. Not all people who kill are cruel.

_____ 4. Capital punishment is revenge.

_____ 5. A prisoner is no longer free.

_____ 6. People naturally want to live.

_____ 7. Execution causes more pain to family members.

_____ 8. The death penalty makes society safer.

_____ 9. Execution may teach other people not to commit crimes.

_____ 10. Execution is more expensive than life imprisonment.

DETAILS

1 Match the main ideas from the previous exercise with the details below. Write the number of the main idea next to the detail. Note that some details support the same main idea. Use your notes to help you.

_____ 1. Some murders are mistakes, caused by anger or fear.

_____ 2. The government spends millions of tax dollars on execution decisions.

_____ 3. Most people would rather go to prison than be executed.

_____ 4. It is hard to wait for a government's decision to execute your loved one.

_____ 5. The message of execution is that murderers will not be allowed to live.

_____ 6. The government can make mistakes when it decides if a person is guilty or not.

_____ 7. Prisoners have the basic pleasures of eating and sleeping.

_____ 8. Executing the murderer is a violent act.

_____ 9. Prisoners cannot do what they want.

_____ 10. Execution stops the murderer from killing again.

2 Look at your notes and at your answers in Preview. How did they help you understand the editorials?

Inferring Both Sides of a Debate

An **inference** is an educated guess about something that is not directly stated in a text. Writers sometimes use arguments to support their opinions in a disagreement. An argument is a reason for an opinion. One kind of argument is a **claim**, or a statement that the writer wants the reader to accept as true. A claim is an opinion that has not been supported by facts. Another kind of argument is **evidence**, which includes examples, facts, and the opinions of experts.

Look at these two arguments from Reading One.

1. "There are times when murder is not committed because of cruelty. People may kill for other reasons, such as anger, misunderstanding, or fear."

2. "Life in prison gives people the chance to improve themselves. Myuran Sukumaran is an example of someone who became a better person in prison. He created museum-quality paintings and helped other prisoners by starting an art school for them."

Are these arguments claims or evidence?

a. Argument 1   claim   evidence

b. Argument 2   claim   evidence

Argument 1 is a claim. The writer wants the reader to agree that prison is better than execution. The writer gives reasons for this argument, but no evidence. Argument 2 mentions Myuran Sukumaran as an example of how people can change in prison. He helped other prisoners by starting an art school for them. Therefore, Argument 2 is evidence.

1 Read the arguments from Reading One and mark each one _C_ (claim) or _E_ (evidence).

_____ a. "Without capital punishment, murderers are allowed to participate in and enjoy life."

_____ b. "There are times when murder is not committed because of cruelty."

_____ c. "It costs the taxpayer millions of dollars more to execute a criminal than to imprison that criminal for life."

_____ d. "Furthermore, the idea that capital punishment stops criminals from committing murder is doubtful: Studies have been unable to show that fear of capital punishment stops someone from committing murder more than other punishments."

2 Use the arguments in Exercise One to complete the chart. First, read each argument in the chart. Then choose which argument from Exercise One gives the opposite opinion. You may write the entire argument or the letter of the argument in the chart.

CAPITAL PUNISHMENT	
PRO: Arguments from Editorial 1	**CON: Arguments from Editorial 2**
1.	Prison is a better form of punishment because it protects society and punishes criminals by taking away their freedom.
2. The people who commit the cruel act of murder give up their rights to citizenship and life itself.	
3. Execution . . . sends a strong message to others who might kill: Killers will not be allowed to live.	
4. Why should the tax money of citizens, including the victim's family, keep the killer alive?	

3 Now discuss your answers with a partner. Point out sentences, words, or statements in the editorials that helped you find the answers.

DISCUSS 🔍

Work in small groups. Choose one of the questions. Discuss your ideas. Then choose one person in your group to report the ideas to the class.

USE YOUR NOTES

Use your notes to support your answers with information from the reading.

1. After reading both editorials, has your opinion changed? If so, which editorial influenced your opinion the most?

2. Which examples are given to support the idea that capital punishment is better for society? Which examples are given to support the idea that prison can change people for the better? How common do you think these examples are?

3. Review the arguments in both editorials. Which do you think is the strongest pro argument? Which is the strongest con argument?

🔷 Go to **MyEnglishLab** to give your opinion about another question.

READING TWO | Charts: Global Facts About Capital Punishment

PREVIEW

1 Look at the title of each chart and the graphics below. What information do you think you will learn in each one?

_____

_____

_____

_____

_____

READ

1 Read the charts. As you read, guess the meanings of the words that are new to you. Remember to take notes on main ideas and details.

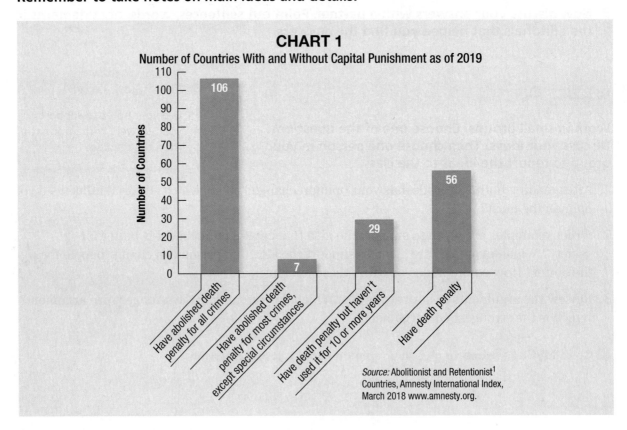

CHART 1

Number of Countries With and Without Capital Punishment as of 2019

Source: Abolitionist and Retentionist[1] Countries, Amnesty International Index, March 2018 www.amnesty.org.

---

[1] **retentionist:** recommending that the death penalty continue

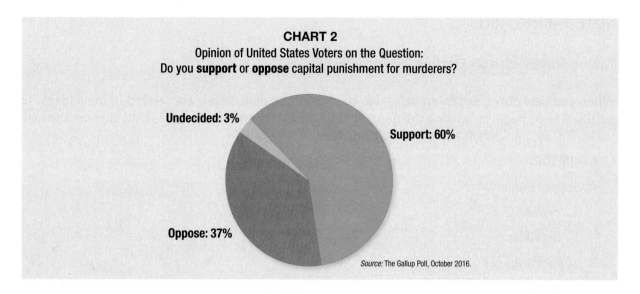

CHART 2
Opinion of United States Voters on the Question:
Do you **support** or **oppose** capital punishment for murderers?

Undecided: 3%

Support: 60%

Oppose: 37%

Source: The Gallup Poll, October 2016.

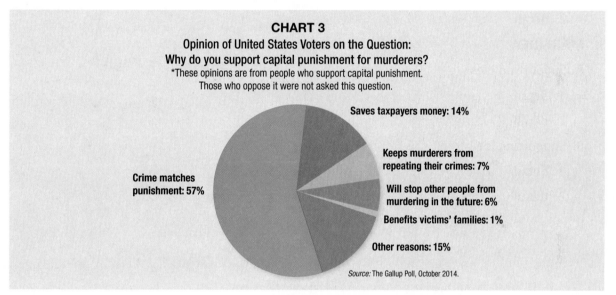

CHART 3
Opinion of United States Voters on the Question:
Why do you support capital punishment for murderers?
*These opinions are from people who support capital punishment.
Those who oppose it were not asked this question.

Saves taxpayers money: 14%

Keeps murderers from
repeating their crimes: 7%

Crime matches
punishment: 57%

Will stop other people from
murdering in the future: 6%

Benefits victims' families: 1%

Other reasons: 15%

Source: The Gallup Poll, October 2014.

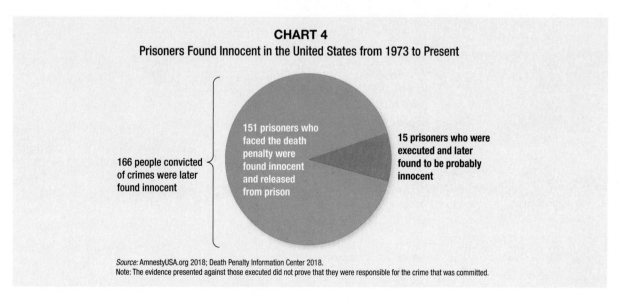

CHART 4
Prisoners Found Innocent in the United States from 1973 to Present

166 people convicted
of crimes were later
found innocent

151 prisoners who
faced the death
penalty were
found innocent
and released
from prison

15 prisoners who were
executed and later
found to be probably
innocent

Source: AmnestyUSA.org 2018; Death Penalty Information Center 2018.
Note: The evidence presented against those executed did not prove that they were responsible for the crime that was committed.

2 **Compare your notes on main ideas and details with a partner's. How can you improve your notes next time?**

Go to the **Pearson Practice English App** or **MyEnglishLab** for more vocabulary practice.

Taking Notes with an Outline

When you take notes, **outlining** helps you to understand how details are related to main ideas. To outline a text, begin by writing the general main ideas. Then write the ideas that support the main ideas. Finally, add details to the supporting ideas.

I. **MAIN IDEA**

    A. Supporting idea

        1. detail

        2. detail

    B. Supporting idea

        1. detail

        2. detail

II. **MAIN IDEA**

    A. Supporting idea

        1. detail

        2. detail

    B. Supporting idea

        1. detail

        2. detail

1 Complete the outline with information from Reading Two.

I. Capital Punishment (WORLD)

    A. Countries that have abolished it for all or most crimes

        1. All crimes: _____

        2. Most crimes: _____

    B. Countries that have retained it

        1. Have retained it but haven't _____ it in 10+ years: _____

        2. Have retained it: _____

II. Capital Punishment (U.S.)

    A. How many Americans support it?

        1. _____

    B. What's the main reason for supporting it? (57%)

        1. _____

    C. What may be a problem with it?

        1. Execution of innocent: probably _____ since 1973

2 Look at Reading Two again. Mark the information you think is most important. Then review your outline. Make sure you understand how details are related to main ideas.

⬤ Go to **MyEnglishLab** for more note-taking practice.

1 Answer the questions. Use your notes from Reading Two to help you. Discuss your answers with a partner.

1. **Chart 1:** When were these facts published?

2. **Chart 1:** How many countries with the death penalty haven't used it in the last 10 years?

3. **Charts 2 and 3:** What conclusion can you make from these charts?

4. **Chart 4:** What does this information show about the capital punishment system in the United States?

5. **Chart 4:** Is this information more likely to be used by someone who supports or opposes capital punishment? Why?

2 Review the boldfaced words from the reading with a partner. Use a dictionary or ask your teacher for any meanings you still do not know.

READING SKILL

1 Look at Reading Two again. How many types of charts are there? Why do you think different types of charts are included?

Identifying Key Information in Charts

Writers use charts and graphs to present numbers and facts clearly. When reading charts and graphs, remember that titles, captions, and notes all contain important information. It is also important to notice the source of information. Study this information in order to interpret the charts and graphs correctly.

> Look at Charts 2 and 3. What is the source of these charts? Which one is more recent? How do you know?

The source of both charts is The Gallup Poll. In Chart 2, the date is October 2016. In Chart 3, the date is October 2014. This is how we know that Chart 2 is more recent.

2 Look at the charts and answer the questions.

1. Look at Chart 1. Do most of these countries support or oppose the death penalty? Explain.

2. Look at Chart 4. How many prisoners have been released since 1973? Why? How many innocent prisoners may have been executed?

3. Identify the main idea of each chart. Look at the example below for Chart 1.

Example:

142 countries have either abolished the death penalty for most crimes or not used it for 10 years, and 56 countries still have the death penalty.

Go to **MyEnglishLab** for more skill practice.

CONNECT THE READINGS 🔍

ORGANIZE

This information is from Reading One (R1) and Reading Two (R2). Write each sentence in the correct column in the pro and con chart.

USE YOUR NOTES

Review your notes from Reading One and Two. Use the information in your notes to complete the chart.

1. It is difficult for the government to decide who is innocent.

2. Murderers in prison have basic pleasures, such as eating and sleeping.

3. Since 1973, 15 prisoners who were probably innocent were executed.

4. Studies do not show that fear of execution stops people from murdering.

5. The victims of murder no longer enjoy the pleasures of life.

6. Since 1973, 151 prisoners who faced the death penalty were found innocent and released from prison.

7. Execution stops the killer from killing again.

8. Execution sends a strong message not to kill.

9. It is unfair that a taxpayer must support the murderer's life in prison.

10. We should stop using the death penalty because of its higher cost.

CAPITAL PUNISHMENT	
Pro Arguments	**Con Arguments**

SYNTHESIZE

Work with a partner. Complete the outlines, listing the pros and cons of capital punishment. Use sentences from Organize.

PRO: Death Penalty

I. It is unfair that a murderer should enjoy life while the victim cannot.

    A. Murderers in prison have basic pleasures, such as eating and sleeping.

    B. _____

II. Execution brings justice and safety.

    A. It is unfair that a taxpayer must support the murderer's life in prison.

    B. _____

    C. _____

CON: Death Penalty

I. Execution may cause an innocent person to die.

    A. Since 1973, 15 prisoners who were probably innocent were executed.

    B. _____

    C. _____

II. Execution is expensive and does not stop murder.

    A. We should stop using the death penalty because of its higher cost.

    B. _____

Go to **MyEnglishLab** to check what you learned.

VOCABULARY

REVIEW

Read the opinion essay written by a student who opposes capital punishment. Complete the sentences with words from the box. Use each word only once.

abolished	forgiveness	innocent	oppose	revenge	support
cruel	guilty	justice	respect	rights	violent

Why I Personally Oppose the Death Penalty

"An eye for an eye" is an expression that is used to support _____. It means
                                                          1.

to hurt someone because he or she hurt you. It is always _____. This is what
                                                              2.

the United States government does when it uses capital punishment. Unfortunately, those

who are executed sometimes have not committed a crime or may be killed unfairly for

political reasons. If we are a nation that believes in equality, shouldn't the death penalty be

used fairly? And yet, it is not. This is why the death penalty is a terrible thing. What should

citizens who _____ the death penalty do? The death penalty should be
                                            3.

_____ because it is morally, economically, and socially wrong.
                         4.

The Supreme Court building in Washington, D.C., says, "Equal _____
                                                                    5.

Under Law" because Americans have always believed every person should be treated fairly.

Yet, a government cannot promise that every execution will be fair. This means that

_____ people may be executed as long as they have a fair trial. But this is not
                            6.

justice. We must also not forget that when an innocent person is found

_____, the real killer is still free! This should not continue.
                         7.

The death penalty uses a lot of the state's money. According to the Miami Herald, it costs

two to six times more to execute a criminal than to imprison him or her for life. Furthermore,

life in prison is better because it gives two benefits: Society is protected from future crime, and

the murderer can think about what he or she has done. Even if the killer doesn't change, the

government has saved a lot of money.

Continued on next page

Many people believe that capital punishment is a deterrent, that murderers won't murder if they know they could be punished with the death penalty. But executions do not discourage others from committing murder. Actually, studies show that murders increase after an execution that has been in the news. States that do not have executions have lower murder rates. Countries that do not have capital punishment have lower murder rates. This shows that killing only results in more _____ behavior.

8.

The death penalty not only encourages killing, but it is also morally and economically wrong. A fair trial doesn't always mean that the truth has been identified, and an innocent person can be put to death. The community loses a friend and keeps a killer. The death penalty does not reflect a nation that has _____ for the _____ of the

9.   10.

individual and believes in equality for all. What should those who oppose the death penalty and _____ life imprisonment do? Speak out against an eye for an eye. Be a

11.

person who practices _____.

12.

EXPAND

1 Nouns that refer to ideas or feelings are called *abstract nouns*. Unlike an *apple*, which is a physical object, abstract nouns, like *love* and *peace*, are ideas that can't be seen or touched. Mark the abstract nouns with *A*. Discuss your answers with the class.

_____ 1. prison	_____ 6. justice	_____ 11. person
_____ 2. friends	_____ 7. family	_____ 12. government
_____ 3. misunderstanding	_____ 8. food	_____ 13. guilt
_____ 4. anger	_____ 9. citizenship	_____ 14. society
_____ 5. punishment	_____ 10. innocence	_____ 15. rights

2 When writers use abstract nouns, they often include examples to help the reader understand more clearly what they mean. Connect the abstract noun on the left with the correct example on the right.

1. cruelty   a. giving criminals a second chance because they have changed

2. fairness   b. hurting a person or animal for no reason

3. guilt   c. going to jail because a person robbed a bank

4. innocence   d. giving a student a failing grade because he or she cheated on a test

5. forgiveness   e. being released from jail because a person didn't do anything wrong

CREATE

APPLY Write a paragraph to answer the questions about capital punishment. Use at least five of the words from the box. You may change the form of the words.

cruel	guilty	justice	punishment	revenge	society
forgive	innocent	murder	respect	rights	violent

1. What do you predict will happen in the future with laws on capital punishment? Will the death penalty continue to be used in some places?

2. Does your country have the death penalty? Do you agree with it, or would you like to change it?

Go to the **Pearson Practice English App** or **MyEnglishLab** for more vocabulary practice.

GRAMMAR FOR WRITING

1 Read the sentences. Each sentence has a main clause and a dependent clause. A main clause can stand alone. A dependent clause cannot. One kind of dependent clause is a *clause of concession*. Underline the main clause of each sentence. Circle the word or words at the beginning of each clause of concession.

Even though murderers are human beings, their crime of murder takes away their right to live.

1. While there is always the chance that an innocent person could be executed by mistake, such cases are rare.

2. Though some people may be scared of the death penalty, there is no proof that it works better than any other punishment.

3. Despite the fact that murder is a terrible crime, there are several reasons why the death penalty should not be used against murderers.

Adverb Clauses of Concession

Concessions are part of opinion writing. A concession means admitting that the opposite opinion may be partly true or right. The purpose of admitting this is to make your own opinion stronger by explaining what is wrong with the opposite opinion. You want to show the weakness in the opposite opinion.

1. In the example, the clause that begins with *while* is a clause of concession. The writer uses this clause to admit that another point of view may be partly true or right by admitting that many people disagree with capital punishment. However, we know that the author supports capital punishment because of the opinion in the main clause.	<u>While many people disagree with capital punishment</u>, the majority of voters in the United States support it.
2. There are several ways to begin clauses of concession: a) while b) despite the fact that c) in spite of the fact that d) even though e) although Be sure to add a subject and a verb to complete the clause. Always put a comma after a clause of concession at the beginning of a sentence.	a) <u>Despite the fact that no society can manage its system of capital punishment perfectly</u>, there are reasons why the death penalty should still be used. b) <u>Even though it is true that some violent people may not commit murder because they fear capital punishment</u>, this punishment doesn't prevent all murder. c) <u>In spite of the fact that capital punishment is legal in some countries</u>, not everyone agrees with it.
3. Another way to write clauses of concession is to put the main clause before the concession clause. Do not use a comma after a main clause at the beginning of a sentence.	There are reasons why the death penalty should still be used <u>despite the fact that no society can manage its system of capital punishment perfectly</u>.

2 **Read the clauses and decide which one is the concession clause. Add the word or phrase in parentheses to make a clause of concession. Then join the two clauses to write a sentence. Read the sentence carefully and decide if it agrees or disagrees with capital punishment by circling *Pro* or *Con*. More than one answer may be possible.**

1. a. Capital punishment may stop some people from committing murder.

   b. There is no proof that it stops many.

   New sentence: (*even though*) _____

   Pro / Con

2. a. Execution stops murderers from killing again.

   b. It is a violent act of revenge.

   New sentence: (*despite the fact that*) _____

   Pro / Con

3. a. They have lost the right to life because of their crime.

   b. Murderers are human.

   New sentence: (*while*) _____

   Pro / Con

4. a. The death penalty is violent.

   b. It should still be used to stop dangerous killers.

   New sentence (*even though*) _____

   Pro / Con

5. a. Murderers have committed a terrible crime.

   b. They should be given a chance to change in prison.

   New sentence: (*while*) _____

   Pro / Con

6. a. Execution is the only sure way to stop murderers from killing again.

   b. An innocent person might be killed by mistake.

   New sentence (*despite the fact that*) _____

   Pro / Con

3 **APPLY Write six sentences giving your opinion of the death penalty. Use the language below to include clauses of concession. Use a comma where necessary.**

   1. Despite the fact that _____ I think

      _____

   2. While some people think _____ I disagree

      _____

   3. I still believe _____ even though

      _____

   4. Even though murderers _____ they still

      _____

   5. Prison is _____ despite the fact that

      _____

   6. While it is true that _____ the death penalty

      _____

Go to the **Pearson Practice English App** or **MyEnglishLab** for more grammar practice.
Check what you learned in **MyEnglishLab**.

In this unit, you read two editorials about capital punishment: one pro and one con. You also analyzed charts containing data about capital punishment. What do you think of capital punishment?

You are going to *write an essay giving your opinion about capital punishment.* You will write an essay in which you try to convince the reader of your point of view.

For an alternative writing topic, see page 175.

PREPARE TO WRITE: Listing: Supporting Arguments and Concessions

1 **In Grammar, Exercise Three, you wrote sentences of concession about capital punishment. On your own, decide whether you are for or against capital punishment and write your opinion here.**

_____

2 **List reasons why your opinion is right. List reasons why the opposite opinion is wrong.**

Why My Opinion Is Right	Why the Opposite Opinion Is Wrong

WRITE

Writing an Opinion Essay

The purpose of an **opinion essay** is to convince the reader to agree with your point of view. Remember these elements of an effective opinion essay:

Give **reasons** to support your opinion.

Use **concrete details** such as examples, quotations, and statistics to support your reasons.

Make one or two **concessions** to show that the opposite opinion is true or right. This will demonstrate that you have thought about the topic critically and will make your own opinion stronger.

1 **Read the essay. Then discuss the questions in a small group.**

1 In some places, murderers get life in prison for their crimes. In others, they get the death penalty. There is a lot of disagreement about how murderers should be punished. However, I believe that people should get the death penalty for murder, not life in prison.

2 One reason I support the death penalty for murder is that prison is not the worst punishment. Even though life imprisonment may be hard in some ways, all prisoners enjoy the basic pleasures of eating and sleeping. There are also opportunities for prisoners to exercise, take classes, read, and practice religion. Some may even enjoy friendships with each other, or get involved in helping the prison community. Why should a murderer be given all these advantages? If you commit the worst crime, it is only fair that you receive the strongest punishment: death.

3 Another reason is that dangerous prisoners sometimes get released many years after they committed their crime. This can be because laws change. An example of this is a law passed in California in 2018 that allows some criminals convicted of murder to be set free years after their crime. Another example is when society forgets what the criminal did. Kenneth McDuff was arrested for murder after he killed three young people. Later, after spending 20 years in prison, he was released on parole because people had forgotten what he did. He then murdered nine more people before he was caught again. While there are unusual cases, such as Stanley "Tookie" Williams, a killer who was nominated for the Nobel Peace Prize after writing eight children's books about not being violent, such prisoners are extremely unusual. Most murderers who are released from prison are still dangerous individuals, and sometimes are even worse as a result of prison life and the influence of other criminals.

4 While opponents of capital punishment say that it is too risky because an innocent person might be killed by mistake, the courts in my country are very careful to make sure that each execution is fair. Before prisoners are executed, there are many court meetings and discussions, which sometimes continue for years. Despite the fact that this may be expensive, it is a very important process. The government has to decide whether or not to end the life of a human being, and when making such a serious decision, it is wise to go slowly. Achieving justice is a process that requires time and attention. As a result of the court process, execution of the innocent is rare.

5 In conclusion, there are many good reasons to give capital punishment to murderers instead of life in prison. It is the only fair punishment for murder that protects both society and the rights of the innocent. It brings lasting justice to victims and their loved ones. For these reasons, I think that the death penalty is a better punishment for murder than life imprisonment.

1. Which sentence is the thesis statement? Remember that a thesis statement states the main idea of the essay and is often the last sentence of the introduction paragraph. What is the writer's opinion?

2. What three reasons support the writer's point of view?

3. What specific examples or details support each reason?

4. What concessions are included? Underline three.

5. Is there a conclusion? Does it repeat the thesis statement?

2 **Look again at what you checked in your list of reasons either for or against capital punishment in Prepare to Write, page 168.**

1. Choose the two reasons that most strongly support your point of view.

2. Choose a strong reason that is opposite to your point of view.

3. Make notes about examples that support your first two reasons.

4. Make notes for concession to the opposite opinion. Be sure to prove that your opinion is stronger.

3 **Now plan the first draft of your essay by completing this outline. Use your notes to help you.**

I. Introductory Paragraph:

Thesis Statement (your opinion about capital punishment):

_____

_____

II. Body Paragraph:

Topic sentence for reason 1:

_____

_____

Supporting Details:

_____

_____

_____

III. Body Paragraph:

Topic sentence for reason 2:

_____

_____

Supporting Details:

_____

_____

_____

IV. Body Paragraph:

Topic sentence for concession:

_____

_____

Supporting Details (for your opinion):

_____

_____

_____

V. Concluding Paragraph:

Restatement of thesis:

_____

Summary of topic sentences of supporting paragraphs:

_____

4 Look at your outline and your notes from Prepare to Write, page 168. Write the first draft of your opinion essay.

- Make sure to include reasons and examples to support your view and the opposing view.

- Use adverb clauses of concession to explain the opposing view.

REVISE: Using Sentence Variety

1 Read the paragraph. Look at the sentences carefully. How are they connected to each other? What kinds of connecting words are used?

Murder is totally unfair because the victims of murder are gone forever. Their hopes and plans have ended permanently, and the pleasures they enjoyed in life have been destroyed. They will never see their friends again and will never hear the voices of their parents, brothers, and sisters. But the murderer is still alive. If we stop capital punishment, murderers will still be allowed to participate in life.

Writers often use different **sentence types** to make their writing more interesting. The three basic **sentence types** are **simple**, **compound**, and **complex**.

1. A **simple sentence** includes one subject and one verb.

   [S]   [V]
   The victims of murder are gone forever.

   A simple sentence can also include a **compound subject**. This is a subject with two or more nouns.

   [S]   [S] [V]
   Their hopes and plans have ended permanently.

2. A **compound sentence** consists of two independent clauses (subject-verb combinations). They are often joined with **coordinating conjunctions (*and, but, or, so*)**.

   [S] [V]   [S]   [V]
   I believe in capital punishment, **but** my sister doesn't.

   A **comma** is used before the coordinating conjunction.

   [S] [V]   [S]   [V]
   You are either in favor of the death penalty, **or** you are against it.

3. A **complex sentence** includes two clauses: independent and dependent. The independent clause (I.C.) is a complete sentence. It can stand alone. The dependent clause (D.C.) begins with a **subordinating conjunction (*if, because, although*)**. The dependent clause is an incomplete sentence. It cannot stand alone.

   [I.C.]   [D.C.]
   Some people believe in capital punishment **if** someone commits murder.

   A **comma** is used when the sentence begins with a dependent clause. It is not used when the sentence begins with an independent clause.

   [D.C.]   [I.C.]
   If we stop capital punishment, murderers will still be allowed to participate in life.

   [I.C.]   [D.C.]
   Murderers will still be allowed to participate in life **if we stop capital punishment**.

2 Read the sentences describing the life of a prisoner, Wayne Paulson. Combine each pair of sentences into one compound or complex sentence. Use coordinating conjunctions (*and, but, or, so*) in compound sentences. Use subordinating conjunctions (*because, if, although*) in complex sentences. Be sure to use subject pronouns and commas where appropriate.

Example:

   a. Wayne reads books in prison.

   b. Wayne sometimes exercises.

   (or)

   Wayne reads books in prison, or he sometimes exercises.

1. a. Wayne was the kind of person who was never noticed at school.

   b. Wayne wasn't the kind of person who got into trouble.

   (and)

   _____

   _____

2. a. Wayne was found guilty at the end of his trial.

   b. He was given the death penalty.

   (because)

   _____

   _____

3. a. Wayne said that he was innocent.

   b. The jury didn't believe Wayne.

   (but)

   _____

   _____

4. a. Wayne still remembers his life before jail.

   b. Wayne's life in jail is very different now.

   (although)

   _____

   _____

5. a. Wayne's mother doesn't want him to feel lonely.

   b. She visits him almost every day.

   (so)

   _____

   _____

3 **Read a Reddit post by an American college student taking a criminal justice class. Rewrite the post to use a variety of sentences: simple, compound, and complex. Make at least five changes, and change the sentence structure as much as you like.**

4.3k

Justice for All ● Posted by innocent_til_proven_guilty 5 hours ago

I'm taking a criminal justice class right now. We've been discussing capital punishment. I have really been shocked by some of the statistics we've learned! Did you know that only four countries account for 84 percent of all executions worldwide? I used to agree with capital punishment. I always thought that the fear of the death penalty stopped some criminals. That is false. Here is a quote I discovered: "Research has failed to provide proof that executions stop murders more than life imprisonment." But the fact that is the most difficult for me to accept is that since 1973, 151 criminals who were sentenced to death were later found to be innocent. Fifteen of those criminals were actually executed. That is a problem that always exists with capital punishment. Some of the prisoners are innocent. They get executed. There is no perfect way to find out if someone is guilty. I now disagree with capital punishment.

4 Look back at the first draft of your essay.

- Make sure you use a variety of sentence types (simple, compound, and complex) to make your writing more interesting.

- Try to use the grammar and some of the vocabulary from the unit.

 Go to **MyEnglishLab** for more skill practice.

EDIT: Writing the Final Draft

APPLY Write the final draft of your paragraph and submit it to your teacher. Carefully edit it for grammatical and mechanical errors, such as spelling, capitalization, and punctuation. Consider how to apply the vocabulary, grammar, and writing skills from the unit. Use the checklist to help you.

FINAL DRAFT CHECKLIST

☐ Does your essay clearly explain the reasons to support your opinion on capital punishment?

☐ Does it contain an introductory paragraph, three body paragraphs, and a concluding paragraph?

☐ Does the introductory paragraph contain a thesis statement stating the main idea of the essay?

☐ Do the first two body paragraphs focus on reasons?

☐ Does each body paragraph contain reasons, examples, and facts to support your opinion?

☐ Does the concluding paragraph restate the main idea expressed in the thesis statement?

☐ Do you use sentence variety to make your writing more interesting?

☐ Do you use clauses of concession?

☐ Do you use vocabulary from the unit?

ALTERNATIVE WRITING TOPIC

APPLY At times, people who visit foreign countries have trouble with the law. When they are punished, they sometimes receive much stronger punishments than they would in their home countries. Do you believe that people who commit crimes in other countries should be punished following the laws of their home country or of the country they're visiting? Write an opinion essay giving your point of view. Use the grammar and vocabulary from the unit.

CHECK WHAT YOU'VE LEARNED

Check (✔) the outcomes you've met and vocabulary you've learned. Put an X next to the skills and vocabulary you still need to practice.

Learning Outcomes
☐ Infer both sides of a debate
☐ Take notes with an outline
☐ Identify key information in charts
☐ Use adverb clauses of concession
☐ Use sentence variety
☐ Write an opinion essay

Vocabulary
☐ abolish
☐ cruel
☐ forgiveness
☐ guilty
☐ innocent
☐ justice
☐ murderer

☐ oppose
☐ respect (*n.*)
☐ revenge
☐ right (*n.*)
☐ society
☐ support
☐ violent

Go to **MyEnglishLab** to watch a video about the death penalty, access the Unit Project, and take the Unit 7 Achievement Test.

LEARNING OUTCOMES

> Infer purpose

> Take notes with symbols

> Identify cohesive devices of contrast

> Use future modals

> Use conjunctions and transitions to show cause and effect

> Write a cause-and-effect essay

🔊 Go to **MyEnglishLab** to check what you know.

Is Our Climate Changing?

1 FOCUS ON THE TOPIC

1. What are some ways Earth is changing?

2. Are humans responsible for changes on the planet? In what ways and to what degree are they responsible?

3. Are these changes making the world better or worse?

VOCABULARY

1 Look at the pictures and read the explanations. Pay attention to the boldfaced words.

How Greenhouse Gases Cause Climate Change

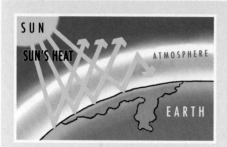

Most of the sun's heat hits the Earth and **escapes** back into space. Some of the heat is trapped by the **atmosphere** and warms the Earth.

When **fossil fuels**, such as coal and gasoline, are burned, **carbon dioxide** (CO_2) is released. Released CO_2 and other **gases** are called greenhouse gas **emissions**.

Greenhouse gases make the atmosphere thicker. As the sun's heat hits the Earth, more and more of the heat is trapped and warms our planet. As CO_2 increases, so does the temperature. This shows that there is a **link** between CO_2 and temperature. This connection is **evidence** that climate change is caused by humans.

Signs of Climate Change
Can we **adapt** to these changes?

More **energetic** weather

Storms, on land and in the ocean, will continue to increase in strength and frequency.

Increasing drought

Countries around the world will be forced to reduce water usage and come up with new ways to farm that use less water.

Rising sea levels and floods

Coastal areas will be at increasing risk as sea levels continue to rise. Some small island nations may soon be entirely covered by water.

2 Choose the best definition for each word or phrase.

1. **escape**

   a. to get out

   b. to change

2. **atmosphere**

   a. mixture of gases that surround the Earth

   b. half of a large sphere

3. **fossil fuels**

   a. a substance (such as coal or oil) that is formed in the ground and can be burned for power

   b. an energy source that comes from the heat of the sun

4. **carbon dioxide** (CO_2)

   a. colorless gas breathed out by people and animals

   b. gas used to produce power in cars, trucks, etc.

5. **gases**

   a. hot air

   b. air-like substances

6. **emissions**

   a. substances that are sent out into the air

   b. representatives of something

7. **link**

   a. effect of something

   b. connection holding two things together

8. **evidence**

   a. interest in something

   b. information that proves something

9. **energetic**

   a. visible

   b. powerful

10. **adapt**

    a. to change something to be used in a different way

    b. to move something so that it is closer to something else

Go to the **Pearson Practice English App** or **MyEnglishLab** for more vocabulary practice.

Look at the title and the subtitles of the article on climate change. Why do you think someone wrote this? Check (✓) one of the answers.

☐ a. to explain what causes climate change

☐ b. to get people to change their lifestyle

☐ c. to warn us about the effects of climate change

READ

1 Read the article about climate change. Create a chart like the one below to take notes. On the left, put the main ideas. On the right, put the details.

TAKE NOTES

Main Ideas	Details
Climate changing	Humans put gases into atmosphere
CO_2 = carbon dioxide	Before 1900: 270–280 ppm
CO_2 = biggest effect, most important to decrease	Now: 408 ppm

Go to **MyEnglishLab** to view example notes.

GLOBAL CLIMATE CHANGE

Increasing Temperatures in the Atmosphere
Earth's **atmosphere** is made up of **gases**; some are warm and some are cool. These gases have always been there and are important because the balance of these cooling and warming gases keeps our weather comfortable and livable. Over the past 50 years, scientists have discovered that the atmosphere is getting hotter because more warming gases are being released, which is changing the balance of warm and cool gases.

Carbon dioxide (CO_2) is an example of a warming gas. The atmosphere needs some CO_2 to provide a balance to the cool gases. CO_2 is released naturally through humans and animals breathing as we breathe in oxygen and breathe out CO_2. However, it is also released through the burning of **fossil fuels**, like coal and gasoline. One hundred years ago, before humans began driving cars and increasing factory production, carbon dioxide accounted for about 275 parts per million (ppm) of all atmospheric gas. Today, the amount of CO_2 in the atmosphere is approximately 408 ppm. This increase in CO_2 **emissions** has affected the balance of warm and cool gases, and now the atmosphere is getting hotter. As the atmosphere gets hotter, it also becomes thicker, making it difficult for these warming gases to **escape**. This means the warming gases are trapped in our atmosphere, where they will continue to increase temperatures.

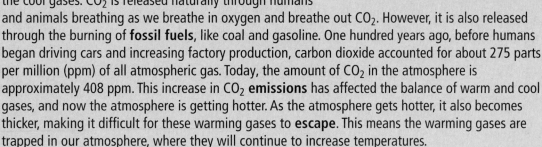

Continued on next page

A Changing Climate

As the atmosphere is getting hotter, the temperature on the planet is increasing as well. This rise in temperature is causing big changes across the globe, changes which are **evidence** that the climate has been affected. Nearly all climate scientists agree that the **link** between higher levels of atmospheric CO_2 and the increase in global temperatures is connected to human activity. They predict that, even if we can greatly reduce CO_2 emissions, temperatures will continue to rise for at least another hundred years.

Effects of Climate Change

As Earth's temperatures continue to rise, the changes to our climate will become more and more severe. We can expect more examples of **energetic** weather. Because stronger storms will bring heavy winds, floods, and massive damage to cities and towns around the world, they will also cause many injuries and deaths. Not only will summers be longer and hotter than ever before, winters will bring record-breaking low temperatures. People living in parts of the world most affected by extreme heat and cold may struggle to **adapt**. Consequently, in order to survive, these people will have to move to areas with more stable climates.

The increasing temperatures are already causing the melting of glaciers, which is resulting in rising sea levels. This is a catastrophic[1] effect that threatens islands and coastal areas across the globe. Along with problems of too much water in some parts of the world, other parts will experience the exact opposite: not enough water. High temperatures combined with long periods of no rains will create drought, causing terrible problems like fires. Hotter temperatures will also affect agricultural production, which could cause global food shortages and famine, which is an extreme lack of food causing death. Clearly, the issue of climate change is very serious, and we all must do our part to slow it before it is too late.

Some Predictions and Results of Climate Change

Most of the world's land is north of the equator, the middle of the Earth. The farther north you go, the warmer and drier it could become. For example, Siberia has always been harsh and cold, but climate change could cause it to become temperate (not too warm and not too cold). It could then become an attractive place to visit. Since the soil of Siberia has never been farmed because it was always covered by snow, it would probably be excellent for farming. Agriculture and tourism could make Russia richer than any other country in the world. In contrast, Pakistan may become too hot for its inhabitants. Temperatures in the Punjab are often over 100°F now, but what if climate change causes the temperature to stay above 120 or 130°F? Another example is the Qori Kalis glacier in Peru. As it melts, it has caused flooding in the valley. As a result, now the valley often has too much water. Eventually, however, the glacier will disappear. When it does, the people in the valley will not have enough water and it will be drier. Finally, Western Europe could begin to experience much colder temperatures as a result of changing ocean temperatures.

Doing Your Part

Governments around the world are taking steps to reduce the amount of CO_2 emissions their countries produce each year. They do this by encouraging the use of vehicles and machines that require less oil or are powered by clean energies, such as wind and solar power, that don't burn fossil fuels. This requires companies to be cleaner and less wasteful. Citizens can also do their part by making small changes to their lives like driving less, using public transportation, or walking. They can also recycle old products and use less electricity in their homes, schools, and workplaces.

These changes will help to reduce the amounts of CO_2 released into the atmosphere, but the effects of the CO_2 that has already been released into our atmosphere will continue to increase temperatures for years to come.

---

[1] **catastrophic:** involving or causing a lot of destruction or suffering

2 Now read the information and the chart about CO_2 emissions.

WORLD EMITTERS[1] OF CARBON DIOXIDE

In order to understand the seriousness of the gas emissions problem, it's helpful to look at how much is being produced and which countries are the biggest producers. This chart shows the percentage of total emissions that were produced by the top 15 emitters in 2016.

TOP 15 EMITTERS OF CARBON DIOXIDE

Rank	Country	Percentage of total emissions
1	China	26.3
2	United States	14.36
3	European Union	9.66
4	India	6.65
5	Russia	5.03
6	Japan	3.09
7	Brazil	2.33
8	Indonesia	1.70
9	Canada	1.69
10	Mexico	1.68
11	Iran	1.64
12	South Korea	1.54
13	Australia	1.33
14	Saudi Arabia	1.25
15	South Africa	1.17

Source: World Resources Institute, 2017.

[1] **emitters:** countries that make emissions

MAIN IDEAS

Write *T* (true) or *F* (false) for each statement. Rewrite the false statements to make them true. Use your notes to help you.

_____ 1. The increase in carbon dioxide is related to our temperature changes.

_____ 2. All places on Earth are getting warmer.

_____ 3. We can stop global warming if we act now.

_____ 4. Human activity contributes to the warming of the Earth.

1 Match the beginning of each sentence on the left with the best ending on the right. Some sentences have more than one correct answer. Use your notes to help you.

_____ 1. Our climate is changing because . . .

_____ 2. An increase in CO_2 shows . . .

_____ 3. Even if we could greatly reduce greenhouse gases, . . .

_____ 4. The largest emitters of CO_2 are . . .

_____ 5. As the atmosphere gets more energetic . . .

_____ 6. Water vapor and greenhouse gases warm the Earth because . . .

_____ 7. Since 1900, . . .

_____ 8. Greenhouse gases are released into the atmosphere when . . .

_____ 9. The earth will be warmer on average, but . . .

a. China, the United States, and the European Union.

b. they allow the heat of the sun in but stop some of the heat from escaping.

c. we burn coal and gasoline.

d. that our atmosphere is changing.

e. it won't be warmer everywhere.

f. the amount of CO_2 in the atmosphere has increased.

g. we will see stronger storms.

h. humans have put a lot of gases into the atmosphere.

i. the world would continue heating for about another 100 years.

2 Look at your notes and at your answers in Preview. How did they help you understand the article?

MAKE INFERENCES 🔍

Inferring Purpose

An **inference** is an **educated guess** about something that is **not directly stated** in a text. A strong **reader can understand the writer's purpose** even though the writer does not say it directly.

Look at the example and read the explanation.

> "One hundred years ago, before humans began driving cars and increasing factory production, carbon dioxide accounted for about 275 parts per million (ppm) of all atmospheric gas. Today, the amount of CO_2 in the atmosphere is approximately 408 ppm."

What is the writer's purpose?

a. To warn the reader about climate change

b. To make comparisons by looking at two or more things to see how they are similar or different

c. To give scientific evidence that climate change is a growing problem

(The best answer is **c**.)

The text **teaches** us **facts** about greenhouse gases and climate change. The reader learns how the earth gets warmer.

After reading the text closely, we can **infer** that the **purpose** of the text is **to give scientific evidence** about climate change.

(continued on next page)

Look at another example and read the explanation.

> Signs of Climate Change: more energetic weather, heavy winds, floods, and massive damage to cities and towns

What is the purpose of this text?

a. To warn the reader about climate change

b. To make comparisons by looking at two or more things to see how they are similar or different

c. To give scientific evidence that climate change is a growing problem

*(The best answer is **a**.)*

The text warns us about situations brought about by climate change that could be **dangerous** and perhaps deadly.

After reading the text closely, we can **infer** that the purpose of the text is **to warn** us about climate change.

1 Look at some important ideas from Reading One. Match each idea with its purpose.

Ideas	Purposes
_____ 1. Increasing Temperatures in the Atmosphere	a. To warn the reader about climate change
_____ 2. Some Predictions and Results of Climate Change	b. To make comparisons by looking at two or more things to see how they are similar or different
_____ 3. World Emitters of Carbon Dioxide	c. To give scientific evidence that climate change is a growing problem

2 Now discuss your answers with a partner. Point out words, phrases, or statements that helped you find the answers.

DISCUSS 🔍

Work in small groups. Choose one of the questions. Discuss your ideas. Then choose one person in your group to report the ideas to the class.

> **▎USE YOUR NOTES**
>
> Use your notes to support your answers with information from the reading.

1. Based on the reading, what are some ways that climate change may create short-term benefits for some parts of the world? Have you observed any short-term benefits of a changing climate?

2. The reading explains some ways that citizens can help to reduce CO_2 emissions: driving less, recycling, etc. What are some things that you do to help? That you don't do?

◗ Go to **MyEnglishLab** to give your opinion about another question.

READING TWO | Solving the Problems of Climate Change

1 Look at the photo below and the title on the next page. Read the first paragraph. Write two questions that you think will be answered in this reading.

_____

_____

2 Look at the boldfaced words in the reading. Which words do you know the meaning of?

READ

1 Read the editorial about climate change. As you read, guess the meanings of the words that are new to you. Remember to take notes on main ideas and details.

2 After you finish reading, compare your notes on main ideas and details with a partner's. How can you improve your notes next time?

SOLVING THE PROBLEMS OF CLIMATE CHANGE

1 Many of us agree that climate change is a major problem in the world today and the **effects** of it are all around us. All across the globe, there are energetic weather patterns that are unlike anything we have ever experienced in human history. Extremely high and low temperatures are being **recorded** around the world every month. In 2018, Dubai, a city in the United Arab Emirates with a desert climate, had the coldest April in history. As climate change continues, every nation in the world is going to experience problems in the very near future. However, the effects of climate change will be especially hard for people living in the poorest nations. In my opinion, people in the world's richer countries must help those in poorer nations, the ones who face the greatest risks of climate change.

2 One effect of climate change is that some areas of the Earth are getting warmer. As temperature averages continue to rise, there will be an increase in extreme weather and natural disasters. These dangers often occur in the southern half of our planet, which will continue to be hit the hardest by storms, tidal waves,[1] and other effects of climate change. This southern area, also known as the tropical part of the Earth, is much hotter than the northern area. Most of the world's poorest nations are in the south, while many of the world's richest nations are in the north. These poor countries, which have not done very much to cause climate change, are suffering the most because of it. For example, Bangladesh, which has a very low emission of greenhouse gases (0.1%), has been facing some of the biggest problems caused by climate change: stronger storms, more flooding, and a decrease in sea life, which has already negatively affected the nation's economy and food supply. It is already hard for countries in the southern part of the world to pay for the basic needs of citizens, such as food, medicine, and education. How can these countries pay for the

3 extra costs that will come with the problems created by climate change?

In addition, people in many of the world's poorest nations depend on farming to make money. As weather changes, the work of farmers will have to change as well, and many farmers will have a hard time adapting to these changes. **Floods** and **droughts** could destroy a whole year's work for an entire nation. This will cause major economic problems for these countries. One problem is **hunger**, a lack of food that **affects** safety and education. In Somalia, temperatures have been rising for 30 years, and this has resulted in more frequent droughts. Consequently, farmers in this poor country have been fighting each other for land. In 2017, more than a million Somali children did not have enough food. How can starving children get a

4 good education, be successful, and build their country's future?

To conclude, we see clearly that the wealthier countries of the world have caused the problems of climate change. Back in the 1800s, when richer countries of the world were starting to build factories and use cars, they were also beginning to emit more and more carbon dioxide. The danger they created for the Earth was a direct result of their efforts to become rich. Centuries later, it is not fair that poorer countries such as Bangladesh and Somalia will have the most problems as a result of climate change. This is a harmful situation that they did not create. While it is clear to scientists that the climate is changing because of humans, not everyone in wealthier nations is worried about these changes. According to Pew Research Center, many people in high carbon-emitting countries, such as the United States, Canada, Australia, and Russia, are not very worried about affecting climate change. The rich people of the north, the ones who have caused climate change, must help countries in the south deal with its consequences.

---

[1] **tidal wave:** a very large ocean wave that flows over the land and destroys things

Go to the **Pearson Practice English App** or **MyEnglishLab** for more vocabulary practice.

Taking Notes with Symbols

When you take notes, using symbols will help you save time. It also takes less space in your notes. Here are some common symbols that can be used for taking notes on any text:

1. because: b/c
2. equals: =
3. does not equal: ≠
4. example: ex
5. and: &
6. money: $
7. increase: ↑
8. decrease: ↓

9. cause and effect: [cause] → [effect]
10. degree: °
11. at: @
12. incorrect: X
13. something important: *
14. with: w/
15. without: w/o

In addition to symbols, you may want to use some abbreviations, such as *info* for *information*, *etc.* for *and so on*, and *vs.* for *against*. If you make up your own abbreviations, be sure to create abbreviations that you will remember later. Here are some examples of how you might use symbols and abbreviations. Look at the first paragraph from Reading Two. Then look at the notes on this paragraph using abbreviations and symbols.

> Many of us agree that climate change is a major problem in the world today and the effects of it are all around us. All across the globe, there are energetic weather patterns that are unlike anything we have ever experienced in human history. Extremely high and low temperatures are being recorded around the world every month. In 2018, Dubai, a city in the United Arab Emirates with a desert climate, had the coldest April in history. As climate change continues, every nation in the world is going to experience problems in the very near future. However, the effects of climate change will be especially hard for people living in the poorest nations. In my opinion, people in the world's richer countries must help those in poorer nations, the ones who face the greatest risks of climate change.

Climate change = major problem

→ ↑ energetic weather

↑ extreme high & low temps

ex: 2018 Dubai = coldest Apr in history

↑ energetic weather → ↑ problems for countries = ↑ problems for poorer countries

1 Take notes on paragraph 2 in Reading Two using symbols.

2 Look at Reading Two again. Mark the information you think is most important.

 Go to **MyEnglishLab** for more note-taking practice.

COMPREHENSION

1 **Answer the questions. Use your notes from Reading Two to help you. Discuss your answers with a partner.**

1. Who will have to deal with the biggest effects of climate change?

   _____

2. As temperatures rise, extreme weather and natural disasters will increase. Where will these events most often occur?

   _____

3. What is one serious economic problem that will happen in the world's poorest nations?

   _____

4. How has education been affected in Somalia?

   _____

5. Which countries have caused most of the climate change in the world? What must they do?

   _____

2 **Review the boldfaced words from the reading with a partner. Use a dictionary or ask your teacher for any meanings you still do not know.**

READING SKILL

1 **Read this quote from Reading Two. Then answer the question.**

> "As climate change continues, every nation in the world is going to experience problems in the very near future. However, the effects of climate change will be especially hard for people living in the poorest nations." *(paragraph 1)*

What information follows the word **however**? What information comes before it?

Identifying Cohesive Devices of Contrast

Writers use **cohesive devices of contrast** to **introduce opposing ideas** in a text. A cohesive device of contrast is a **word or phrase** that tells us that the information that will follow is different from what comes before it. It also introduces a point that the author believes is more important than what comes before it.

Look at the example again and read the explanation.

> • "As climate change continues, every nation in the world is going to experience problems in the very near future. However, the effects of climate change will be especially hard for people living in the poorest nations."

In the first sentence, we learn that **every nation in the world** is going to experience problems in the very near future. In the second sentence, we learn that climate change will be **harder for people in poorer nations.**

The use of the word *however* helps the reader to **expect contrast** (different information), NOT comparison (similar information). Here, the contrast, or difference, is the one between every nation and the poorest nations. Not every nation in the world is poor. *However* is a **cohesive device of contrast** that shows the difference between the poorest nations and every nation in the world.

---

2 **Work with a partner. Read the quotes from Reading One. Underline the cohesive devices that show contrast. What are they contrasting?**

1. "Agriculture and tourism could make Russia richer than any other country in the world. In contrast, Pakistan may become too hot for its inhabitants."

2. "Temperatures in the Punjab are often over 100°F now, but what if climate change causes the temperature to stay above 120 or 130°F?"

3. "As a result, now the valley often has too much water. Eventually, however, the glacier will disappear."

Go to **MyEnglishLab** for more skill practice.

CONNECT THE READINGS

ORGANIZE

A causal chain helps you to see the relationships between causes and effects. A cause-and-effect relationship is when one event makes another event happen. Look at the causal chain describing the information in Reading One (R1) and Reading Two (R2).

> **USE YOUR NOTES**
>
> Review your notes from Reading One and Two. Use the information in your notes to complete the chain.

Look back at the readings and choose the correct causes and effects to complete the causal chain. Notice that, in a causal chain, the effects become the causes of the information that follows.

decrease	energetic	gases	hard	hotter	hunger	poorer	rich

1. Humans put _____ into the atmosphere, including CO_2.

→2. CO_2 makes atmosphere _____.

→3. Atmosphere becomes more _____ = climate change.

→4. It's important to _____ CO_2 because its effect is more than that of other gases.

→5. _____ countries produce more CO_2.

→6. Rising temperature caused by more CO_2 = problems everywhere, especially in the _____ countries of the world.

→7. Poor farmers will have a _____ time.

→8. More _____ and more fighting in poorer countries.

SYNTHESIZE

Use the information in Organize to complete a summary of climate change and its effects on the world.

Many scientists believe that the world's climate is changing because of fossil fuels that humans have put into the atmosphere. When humans put gases such as CO_2 into the atmosphere, _____

_____

This is the process we call climate change. _____

_____

Another concern is that rich countries have put more carbon dioxide into the atmosphere than poorer countries. Rising temperatures _____

_____

_____

○ Go to **MyEnglishLab** to check what you learned.

REVIEW

Read the story about a group called Global Climate Coalition. Complete the story with the words from the box.

adapt	carbon dioxide	emissions	escape	fossil fuels	link
atmosphere	effects	energetic	evidence	gases	recorded

The Global Climate Coalition

The Global Climate Coalition (GCC) was founded in 1987. It was a group that included some of the world's most powerful oil companies, including British Petroleum (BP), Royal Dutch Shell, DuPont, Chevron, Texaco, and the Ford Motor Company. It was created immediately after the Intergovernmental Panel on Climate Change (IPCC) was formed. The purpose of the GCC was to confuse the public about climate change so that the public would not agree to reduce CO_2 emissions, and the GCC was very successful. In 1997, just before the Kyoto Conference on Climate Change, the GCC started a massive advertising campaign. The purpose of this campaign was to stop the United States from agreeing to reduce gas

_____ that _____ from cars and factories. The ads
     1.   **2.**

tried to frighten Americans. They told Americans that if they decreased their use of

_____ , the price of gasoline would go up. They said that one of the
    3.

_____ would be a price increase of 50 cents a gallon. This wasn't true,
    4.

but the advertising was successful!

After the GCC secretly spent 63 million dollars lobbying against environmental issues, their lies began to catch up with them. Finally, the chairman of BP announced in May 1997 that the _____ between greenhouse _____
       5.   **6.**

and climate change was too strong to ignore. BP left the Global Climate Coalition. DuPont, Royal Dutch Shell, and Ford also left later. Ford's decision showed that fossil fuel industries were changing. In 2000, DaimlerChrysler, Texaco, and General Motors left the Coalition, too. Leading companies left the Global Climate Coalition because there was more and more _____ that the _____

7.   8.

was really getting warmer and more _____ . This data, based on

9.

temperatures that were higher than any previously _____ , showed that

10.

_____ was the cause. Members of the GCC wanted to keep everything

11.

the same, while the companies that left were the ones trying to _____

12.

to the new information about climate change. These companies joined a new group called the Business Environmental Leadership Council, as did Toyota and Boeing. Companies that joined the Council had to have their own programs to reduce carbon emissions.

The GCC was disbanded[1] in 2002. The organization responsible for confusing the world about climate change would not publish false science anymore.

_____

[1] **disbanded:** to stop existing as an organization

EXPAND

Look at the list of nouns from Reading One and Reading Two. Which nouns can be used with the adjectives in the exercise? Some nouns can be used more than once.

| atmosphere | climate | emissions | fossil fuels | government |
| carbon dioxide | effects | evidence | gases | storms |

1. successful: _____

2. clear: _____

3. warm: _____

4. stronger: _____

5. energetic: _____

6. harmful: _____

7. increasing: _____

8. national: _____

CREATE

APPLY Write a paragraph explaining how climate change affects you personally. Use at least five of the words from the box. You may change the form of the words.

adapt	atmosphere	drought	evidence	gases
affect	carbon dioxide	effect	floods	government
agreement	climate	emissions	fossil fuels	hunger

Go to the **Pearson Practice English App** or **MyEnglishLab** for more vocabulary practice.

1 **Read the paragraph. Circle the words *may, might, could,* and *will.* Underline the verbs that follow. How do the circled words change the meanings of the verbs?**

> Climate scientists use computers to make models of how the climate might respond to more carbon dioxide in the atmosphere. Some of the changes may be good, and some may be bad. Since the atmosphere is getting more energetic, some places will be warmer, some places will be wetter, and some places will be drier. Some places may even be cooler. Many of the changes will cause shortages of drinking water and food for people and animals, especially in poor countries. But if we could cut emissions by half, we might be able to manage the changes and adapt to them.

Future Modals

1. Use *may, might,* and *could* to talk about future possibility. Remember that *possibility* means that something may or may not happen. It is uncertain.	It **may** be windier. It **might** be drier. It **could** be managed.
2. Use *may not* and *might not* to express the possibility that something will not happen. Use *couldn't* to express the idea that something is impossible. **BE CAREFUL!** We never contract *might not* and *may not*.	There are a lot of clouds, but it **might not** rain. We **couldn't** stop carbon dioxide emissions completely, but we could reduce them. USE: If we develop new fuels, we **may not** need oil in the future. NOT: If we develop new fuels, we ~~mayn't~~ need oil in the future. USE: There are a lot of clouds, but it **might not** rain. NOT: There are a lot of clouds, but it ~~mightn't~~ rain.

(continued on next page)

3. **Questions** about possibility usually do not use *may, might,* or *could*. They use the future (*will, be going to*), the present progressive, or phrases such as *Do you think . . . ?* or *Is it possible that . . . ?*

The **answers** to these questions often use *may, might,* or *could*.

In **short answers** to yes / no questions, use *may, might,* or *could* alone.

Usage Note: If *be* is the main verb, it is usually included in the short answer.

Q: When **will** CO_2 levels **come down**?

A: They **might start** coming down in 100 years.

Q: **Are** we **going to be able** to adapt?

A: We **might adapt** if we limit emissions soon.

Q: When **will** the temperature **stop rising**?

A: It **may stop** in 100 years.

Q: **Do you think** developing countries **will reduce** gas emissions?

A: They **could reduce** them if it's not too expensive.

Q: Will the richer nations of the world help the poorer ones?

A: They **might**.

Q: Will climate change **be slowed**?

A: It **might be**.

4. NOTE: *Will* is used to talk about future certainty, not possibility. To be certain about something means that you are 100 percent sure it will happen. Use *will* when you are certain of something.

Hungry children in poor countries **will** have problems in school. They won't be able to study well.

---

2 **Complete the questions and answers to express future possibility or certainty. Include negative forms. There may be more than one correct answer.**

1. **Q:** What will the weather be like in Siberia in the next 100 years?

   A: It _____ be warm and comfortable.

   a. may

   b. may not

   c. will

2. **Q:** Will all places in the world be wetter in the next 100 years?

   A: They _____ be.

   a. could

   b. will

   c. will not

3. **Q:** When will sea levels stop rising?

   A: Scientists are not sure. Sea levels _____ stop rising in 100 years.

   a. may not

   b. will

   c. may

4. **Q:** Will rich countries help poor ones deal with climate change?

   A: They _____ . It's a complicated problem.

   a. might not

   b. will

   c. will not

5. **Q:** What will happen as temperatures continue to rise?

   A: Scientists are sure that there _____ be an increase in extreme weather and natural disasters.

   a. could

   b. will

   c. will not

6. **Q:** How much stronger do you think hurricanes could get?

   A: They _____ get up to Category 5.

   a. will

   b. might

   c. may not

7. **Q:** What will happen if many hurricanes become Category 5?

   A: If this happens, we _____ be able to deal with the problems that result.

   a will

   b. will not

   c. might not

8. **Q:** Do you think people could deal with a hurricane that is stronger than that?

   A: No. We _____ deal with a hurricane that is stronger—that is impossible!

   a. might

   b. could

   c. could not

3 APPLY **Work with a partner. Make questions about climate change in the place where you are now living using modals. Then interview a partner using your questions. Your partner will use modals in his or her answers. Share your answers with the class.**

▶ Go to the **Pearson Practice English App** or **MyEnglishLab** for more grammar practice. Check what you learned in **MyEnglishLab**.

In this unit, you read a Reddit post and an editorial about climate change.

You are going to *write an essay about how climate change is affecting your home country or another country*. What changes have already occurred? What is changing now? What changes are predicted for the future? Explain the causes and effects of these changes.

For an alternative writing topic, see page 203.

PREPARE TO WRITE: Using a Causal Chain

1 **Look at the causal chains. A causal chain helps you to see the relationships between causes and effects. The arrows show how one or more causes lead(s) to one or more effects. Look at these examples from Reading One.**

> warmer gases → hotter atmosphere
>
> increasing temperatures → melting of glaciers → rising sea levels
>
> high temperatures + no rain → drought → fires

2 **Think of the causes and effects you will be writing about as you describe how climate change is affecting your country or another country. Draw a causal chain to help you organize the cause-and-effect relationships.**

WRITE

Writing a Cause-and-Effect Essay

In a **cause-and-effect essay,** the writer explains the **relationships** between the causes and effects of a situation. Often, there are many causes which result in one effect or one cause which results in many effects.

1 **Read the essay and complete the activities.**

1 The future of climate change does not look very good for our world. There will be flooding of coastlines, water shortages, and food shortages. The areas near the middle of the Earth will suffer the most because they will become hotter and experience more storms and dry weather. The poor will become poorer, and the wealthy will become wealthier. Many of the 54 nations on the continent of Africa will experience the worst effects of climate change due to irregular weather, the rising temperature of the atmosphere and water, and rising sea levels. Because of this, the developed nations of the world that emit the greatest amount of CO_2 need to reduce emissions, and they should support African nations in developing technologies to combat the effects of climate change.

2 The continent of Africa is home to diverse climates, climates that have always been irregular, and now climate change is causing weather that is even more irregular. Dry areas are becoming drier, and wet areas are becoming wetter. In the future, this will hurt people who grow their own food since the time of the growing season and the amount of food they get will decrease. Since 70 percent of people on this continent grow their own food, they will not have enough. In some countries, the amount of food grown could decrease by 50 percent.

(continued on next page)

3 Another problem is the rising temperature of the atmosphere and water. Africa is an average 0.5°F hotter than it was 100 years ago. In some areas, however, it is as much as 3.5°F hotter, and it is believed that it could be 7–9°F hotter in the next 100 years. As a result, the land is becoming drier. Another result is that the glaciers are melting. The snows of Kilimanjaro in Tanzania are expected to disappear in the next 10–20 years. Also, rising water temperatures in lakes will result in fewer fish, another important food. In addition, the rising temperature of the North Atlantic will cause rain to occur further and further north, so that countries in southern Africa will experience less and less rain. This will cause more drought. As this results in more hunger, children will be unable to study well, which might make the future of these countries even worse.

4 In the next 50 to 100 years, there will be flooding of coastlines since sea levels will rise. Populations living along Africa's coastlines will have to move farther inland. These people will have to find new homes or will risk homelessness, and many governments in African nations are not currently prepared to support these displaced people. In addition, some of the best farmland will be under water. This will result in more food shortages, which could cause people to literally have to fight one another for food.

5 The latest studies of climate change show that the risks of climate change are greater on the continent of Africa than in any other part of the world. According to Andrew Simms of the New Economics Foundation, "Global warming is set to make many of the problems which Africa already deals with much, much worse." Unless the developed nations of the world reduce gas emissions now, we could see millions of people die of hunger and sickness. Many scientists and governments in African nations are working to develop technologies to adapt to the changing climate, but they shouldn't have to face this alone. Countries around the world must come together to support the nations of Africa in combating the effects of climate change.

1. Read the introductory paragraph. What is the thesis statement (main idea of the essay)? Underline it.

2. Read paragraph 2 and draw a cause-and-effect map for it.

3. Read paragraph 3 and draw a cause-and-effect map for it.

4. Read paragraph 4 and draw a cause-and-effect map for it.

5. Read paragraph 5. What is the conclusion statement (restatement of the thesis)?

2 Look back at the causal chain you created in Prepare to Write, page 198. Add notes about reasons, examples, and facts to support your causes and effects.

3 Use your causal chain and notes to write the first draft of your cause-and-effect essay.

- Write **an introductory paragraph** including a thesis statement (main idea of your essay) about how climate change is affecting the country you have chosen.

- Include **three body paragraphs**, each one focusing on one set of cause-and-effect relationships. Each body paragraph will give reasons, examples, and facts to support your causes and effects.

- End with **a concluding paragraph** summarizing your main ideas or restating the thesis statement and adding a final comment.

- Use future modals to talk about future possibility.

REVISE: Using Conjunctions and Transitions to Show Cause and Effect

1 Look at the sentences from Reading One. What do the boldfaced words mean?

- **Because** stronger storms will bring heavy winds, floods, and massive damage to cities and towns around the world, they will also cause many injuries and deaths.

- **Since** the soil of Siberia has never been farmed because it was always covered by snow, it will probably be excellent for farming.

- People living in parts of the world most affected by extreme heat and cold may struggle to adapt. **Consequently,** in order to survive, these people will have to move to areas with more stable climates.

- As it melts, it has caused flooding in the valley. **As a result**, now the valley often has too much water.

Conjunctions and Transitions to Show Cause and Effect

Because, since, and *as* are conjunctions that show the cause or reason for something. *Therefore, consequently, thus*, and *as a result* are transitions that show effect. Notice that the transitions showing effect are always followed by a comma. Writers use conjunctions and transitions to help the reader understand causes and effects. These words or phrases prepare the reader for what type of information will come next.

Conjunctions Used to Show Cause

because	since	as

- It's changing **because** humans have put gases into the atmosphere.
- In the next 100 years, there will be flooding of coastlines **since** sea levels will rise.
- We know that the atmosphere is getting more energetic **as** it is getting hotter.

Transitions Used to Show Effect

Therefore,	Consequently,	Thus,	As a result,

- The advertising campaign scared Americans. **Therefore**, they decided they didn't want to reduce gas emissions.
- The Global Climate Coalition was a group that included some of the most powerful oil companies. **Consequently,** it was able to pay for a massive advertising campaign.
- The atmosphere is getting hotter and more energetic. **Thus,** in some places it will be windier, in some places wetter, in some places drier.
- The climate is changing. **As a result,** every country in the world will be affected.

2 **Read this report about climate change around the world. Complete the sentences with the best choice of conjunctions and transitions. You may need to add commas to some sentences.**

According to the IPCC (Intergovernmental Panel on Climate Change), climate change in the next century could bring many problems to different parts of the world. In Africa, up to 400 million people will not have enough water. _____ this will hurt
1. (Since / As a result)

agriculture, or farming, and there will not be enough food. _____
2. (As a result / Because)

more people in Africa will die of hunger. The water temperature of lakes will increase.

_____ there will be fewer and fewer fish to eat, and many people,
3. (Consequently / As)

including children, could be affected.

In Asia, the melting of glaciers will first cause flooding. Later, _____
4. (therefore / as)

the glaciers get smaller, the rivers will dry up. In some areas of Asia, agriculture will improve 20 percent, while in other areas it will decrease by 30 percent. This means that some farmers may become richer, but others will face difficult problems.

There will be less rain in Australia and New Zealand. _____ there
5. (As a result / Since)

will be less water and less clean water. In southern and eastern Australia, there will be drought and fires. In some areas of New Zealand, however, farming will improve because it will be warmer, and there will be more rain. _____ the coastal areas will have
6. (Because / Consequently)

more and bigger storms, there will be more flooding. This may cause many people to lose their homes.

In northern Europe, it will be warmer. _____ agriculture will
7. (Therefore / As)

increase and forests will grow. In southern Europe, there will be drought and water shortages

_____ it will be warmer. People from this area may try to move north.
8. (therefore / since)

In North America, it will be warmer and drier. _____ there will be
9. (As a result / As)

more fires and disease, and problems with insects. _____ some areas
10. (Because / Thus)

will be drier, South America will have a decrease in agriculture. _____
11. (As a result / As)

sea temperatures rise, there will be fewer fish in some places. These things will result in food shortages, which could cause fighting between countries.

3 Now go back to the first draft of your essay.

- Add subordinating conjunctions and cause-and-effect transition signals to help the reader move from one idea to the next. Don't forget to use commas where needed.

- Try to use the grammar and some of the vocabulary from the unit.

▶ Go to **My**English**Lab** for more skill practice.

EDIT: Writing the Final Draft

APPLY Write the final draft of your essay and submit it to your teacher. Carefully edit it for grammatical and mechanical errors, such as spelling, capitalization, and punctuation. Consider how to apply the vocabulary, grammar, and writing skills from the unit. Use the checklist to help you.

FINAL DRAFT CHECKLIST

☐ Does your essay clearly explain the causes and effects that you think are important for your topic?

☐ Does it contain an introductory paragraph, three body paragraphs, and a concluding paragraph?

☐ Does the introductory paragraph contain a thesis statement stating the main idea of your essay?

☐ Does each body paragraph focus on one set of cause-and-effect relationships?

☐ Does each body paragraph contain reasons, examples, and facts to support the causes and effects?

☐ Do you use cause-and-effect transitions to help the reader move from one idea to the next?

☐ Does the concluding paragraph restate the main idea expressed in the thesis statement?

☐ Do you use *may, might, could,* or *will* to express future certainty or possibility?

☐ Do you use new vocabulary from the unit?

ALTERNATIVE WRITING TOPIC

APPLY Imagine you work for a government organization that provides help to victims of natural disasters. Write a report of three or four paragraphs about a natural disaster that you know about. What caused the disaster? What were the results of the disaster? Who helped the victims after it happened? Did the government provide most of the help (relief)? Did international organizations help? How long did it take for this area to recover? Use the grammar and vocabulary from the unit.

CHECK WHAT YOU'VE LEARNED

Check (✔) the outcomes you've met and vocabulary you've learned. Put an X next to the skills and vocabulary you still need to practice.

Learning Outcomes
☐ **Infer purpose**
☐ **Take notes with symbols**
☐ **Identify cohesive devices of contrast**
☐ **Use future modals**
☐ **Use conjunctions and transitions to show cause and effect**
☐ **Write a cause-and-effect essay**

Vocabulary
☐ **adapt** AWL
☐ **affect** AWL
☐ **atmosphere**
☐ **carbon dioxide**
☐ **drought**
☐ **effect**
☐ **emissions**
☐ **energetic** AWL

☐ **escape** (*v.*)
☐ **evidence** AWL
☐ **flood**
☐ **fossil fuels**
☐ **gas**
☐ **hunger**
☐ **link** (*n.*) AWL
☐ **record** (*v.*)

Go to **MyEnglishLab** to watch a video about climate change, access the Unit Project, and take the Unit 8 Achievement Test.

EXPAND VOCABULARY

UNIT 1
Vocabulary

accomplish
accomplishment
challenge (v.) [AWL]
challenging (adj.) [AWL]
complicate
complicated
dare (n.)
dare (v.)
daring (adj.)
daringly
enormously [AWL]
enormousness
focus (n.) [AWL]
focus (v.) [AWL]
impress

impression
impressively
inspiration
inspiring (adj.)
inspiringly
obsess
obsessed (adj.)
obsessive
obsessively
pressure (v.)
pressured (adj.)
risk (v.)
risky
willing
willingly

UNIT 2
Vocabulary

convince [AWL]
convincingly [AWL]
deceive
deceptive
deceptively
duplicate (n.)
duplicate (v.)
duplication
fake (n.)
fake (v.)
fakery

fraudulent
fraudulently
honest
honestly
impersonation
impression
impressive
impressively
motivate [AWL]
motivated (adj.) [AWL]
motivation [AWL]

UNIT 3

Vocabulary

artificial intelligence
automatic pilot
flight simulator

Multi-word Units

establish yourself
isolated incident

UNIT 4
Vocabulary

assert
assertively
domination [AWL]
dominant [AWL]
exceptional
exceptionally
excess
excessively
inferiority
mythical
profane

proverb
proverbial
sexism [AWL]
synonymous
talk
talkativeness
unique [AWL]
uniquely [AWL]
value (n.)
value (v.)

UNIT 5
Vocabulary

beneficial [AWL]
entrepreneurial
expert (adj.) [AWL]
occupational [AWL]

prospective [AWL]
strategic [AWL]
sustainable [AWL]

UNIT 6
Vocabulary
None

UNIT 7
Vocabulary

cruelty
fairness
forgiveness
guilt

innocence
misunderstanding
punishment

UNIT 8
Vocabulary
None

ACADEMIC WORD LIST VOCABULARY AWL

Words with an * are target vocabulary in the unit. The remainder of the words appear in context in the reading texts.

achieve
adapt*
affect* (v.)
analyze
appreciate
approximately
area
assignment
assistant
attitude
authority
automatically*
available
aware
beneficial*
benefit* (n.)
capable
category
challenge* (v.)
challenge*(n.)
challenging* (adj.)
chapter
chart
chemical
circumstances
commit
communicate
communication
community
complex
comprehensive
computer
conclude
consequence*
consequently*
constantly
contact (n.)
contract (n.)

convince*
convincing* (adj.)
convincingly*
create
credit (n.)
cultural
culture
data
decade
definitely
depression*
design (n.)
designer (n.)
despite
document (n.)
dominant*
dominate*
domination*
economic
edit
energetic*
energy
enormous*
enormously*
ensure*
environment
environmental
equipment
establish*
evaluate
eventually
evidence*
exclude
expert* (adj.)
expert* (n.)
federal
file (v.)
final

finally
finances (n.)
financial
focus* (n.)
focus* (v.)
focused* (adj.)
gender
generation
global
globe
goal
identify
immigration
injured* (adj.)
injury
innovator
instance
institution
intelligence
investigate
involve
isolated* (adj.)
issue (n.)
issue (v.)
item
job
legal
license (n.)
licensed (adj.)
likewise
link* (n.)
locate
location
major (adj.)
media
medical
mental
method

military
motivate*
motivated* (adj.)
motivation*
motive*
negative
normal
obtain
occupational*
occur
option
partner
percent
percentage
period
physical
plus (v.)
predict
prediction
primarily
principle (n.)
process (n.)
professional
project (n.)

prospect*
prospective*
psychologist
purchase (n.)
purchase (v.)
reaction*
regional
release (v.)
release (n.)
rely
require
research (v.)
research* (n.)
resident
resource
respond
role
schedule
security*
select
series
sexism*
similar
similarity

simulate*
specific
stable
statistics
strategic*
strategy*
stress (n.)
stressed (adj.)
survive*
sustainability
sustainable*
team
technology
temporary
topic
traditional
transportation
uniform (n.)
unique*
uniquely*
uniqueness*
vehicle

GRAMMAR BOOK REFERENCES

NorthStar: Reading and Writing Level 3, Fifth Edition	Focus on Grammar, Level 3, Fifth Edition	Azar's Basic English Grammar, Fifth Edition
Unit 1 Modals of Ability	**Unit 13** Ability and Possibility: *Can, Could, Be able to*	**Chapter 7** The form of modal auxiliaries: 7-1 Expressing Ability: *can* and *could*: 7-2
Unit 2 Simple Past and Past Progressive	**Unit 2** Simple Past **Unit 3** Past Progressive and Simple Past	**Chapter 2** Expressing Past Time: 2-1, 2-2, 2-3, 2-4, 2-5, 2-6, 2-7, 2-8
Unit 3 Infinitives of Purpose	**Unit 24** Infinitives After Certain Verbs **Unit 25** More Uses of Infinitives **Unit 26** Gerunds and Infinitives	**Chapter 13** Gerunds and Infinitives: 13-1, 13-2, 13-3, 13-4, 13-5, 13-6, 13-7, 13-8, 13-9, 13-10
Unit 4 Comparative Adverbs	**Unit 22** Adverbs: *As . . . as*, Comparatives, Superlatives	**Chapter 9** Comparisons: 9-1, 9-2, 9-3, 9-4, 9-5, 9-6, 9-7, 9-8, 9-9, 9-10, 9-11
Unit 5 Future Time Clauses	**Unit 7** Future Time Clauses	**Chapter 3** Expressing the future in time clauses and *if*-clauses: 3-6
Unit 6 *Because* and *Even Though*		**Chapter 8** Connecting ideas with *because*: 8-6 Connecting ideas with *even though*: 8-7
Unit 7 Adverb Clauses of Concession	**Unit 19** Adjectives and Adverbs **Unit 22** Adverbs	**Chapter 8** Connecting ideas with *even though / although*: 8-7
Unit 8 Future Modals	**Unit 31** Future Possibility: *May, Might, Could* **Unit 32** Present Conclusions: *Must, Have (got) to, May, Might, Could, Can't*	**Chapter 7** The form of modal auxiliaries: 7-1 Expressing possibility: *may, might,* and *maybe*: 7-3 Using *could* to express possibility: 7-4

CREDITS

NOTES

NOTES

NOTES

NOTES